ENEMY IN YOUR POCKET

HOW USING YOUR PHONE LESS WILL CHANGE YOUR LIFE AND HOW TO DO IT

Copyright © 2024 Jackson Antonow

All rights reserved. No party of this book may be reproduced or used in any manner without the prior written permission of the copyright owner, except for the use of quotations for book reviews.

To request permissions, contact the publisher at
jacksonantonowwriting@gmail.com

Paperback: 9798334886094

Library of Congress Number: 2024916781

First Paperback Edition: August 2024

Edited by: Cole Tiran, Andrew Dawson and Ellen Tarlin
Cover Art: Rica Graphics
Photos: William Moriarty
Layout by: Erica Patstone

For all other inquires contact:
jacksonantonowwriting@gmail.com

Thank you to my mom and dad for always supporting me in everything I do and to my friends who provided valuable insights for this book.

Table of Contents

	Introduction	6
1	Addiction	8
2	Why You Should Put Down Your Phone	11
3	The Social Media Business Model	26
4	How Social Media Actually Affects People Today	32
5	Can We Fix Social Media?	45
6	The Phone Beyond Social Media	48
7	Redesign Your Phone	52
8	Changing Our Habits	90
	Conclusion	99
	Acknowledgments	100
	Endnotes	103

Introduction

It was a Monday morning during my freshman year of college, and I did the same thing I had done every morning for the last seven years: I checked my phone for notifications and then sat in bed scrolling aimlessly. The difference that day was I came to the realization that I was depressed. I couldn't be bothered to get out of bed each morning when I had a device that gave me the stimulation that I wasn't getting in the real world. When I finally summoned the strength to get out of bed and face the world, I was constantly glued to my phone. I scrolled before I got to class, during class, when I was with my friends, before I went to bed, and anytime I had the opportunity. I averaged around eight hours a day on my phone. I was in a never-ending cycle of scrolling through apps, and my phone was determining the trajectory of my life. In the rare moments when I looked up from my phone, I could see my world crumbling around me.

On paper, my life looked good: I was accepted into a good university, was in shape physically, had a great group of friends, and my social media portrayed someone who was happy with their life, but it wasn't true. I may have been at a good university, but I was struggling to keep up because I could never get off my phone. I was in shape physically but was constantly insecure about how I looked because I was always comparing myself to others. My friends were great, but I couldn't appreciate them because I was always worried I could be having more fun somewhere else. I was so discontent with my life; I realized I had to make a change. I didn't want to spend the rest of my life feeling depressed and anxious when I didn't have to.

During the second semester of my freshman year, I changed my relationship with my phone and changed my life. I went from averaging around eight hours a day spent on my phone to just an hour. Since I made this change, I wake up extremely grateful every morning in a way I couldn't even describe to my previous self. My feelings of constant anxiety, unhappiness, and inadequacy are completely gone. It almost feels as if I'm living in a different world.

When I started trying to cut my phone usage, there was no outlet to help me. I tried reading books and watching YouTube videos, but they either didn't understand the issue through a teenager's lens, were insufficiently researched, or just couldn't describe how I was feeling. I was forced to draw from many different sources, which resulted in a lot of hiccups along the way.

I sat down to write this book because I believe there is a significant need for it. I wanted to create a source that could help people end their addiction to their phone and improve their life. A book from the perspective of a teenager, with adequate research, that understands the feelings of anxiety and sadness that comes with excessive phone usage.

The way we use our phones is affecting all aspects of our lives, whether that's school, work, our relationships with others, or our mental health. I believe that changing our relationship with our phone is one of the easiest ways to become happier, and more satisfied with our life. Using my phone less transformed the quality of my life and I hope it can do the same for you.

This book will examine the phone addiction issue, the benefits of decreased usage, the multitude of problems with social media, issues outside of social media, and how to get rid you of your phone addiction one step at a time. This isn't advice from a seventy-year-old university researcher with no real experience of being addicted to their phone but from a former addict who had been glued to his phone since he was twelve years old.

Now that I have set the stage, I want to emphasize two points. First, I have only included information that I believe is truly useful. Of the countless other books I have read on this issue, the common theme was pages of information unrelated to phone usage, seemingly included in an attempt to meet a page requirement. I promise you, I will not waste your time.

Second, this book is going to be about **the individual**, about how one person can take the steps to cure their phone addiction. Most of the other books I have read on this topic have been concerned with larger societal change, which is great, but that's not what this book is about. I am not going to call for legislative action or changes in the behavior of parents because, frankly, I don't have that kind of influence—nobody does. And as with any addiction, you can't force people to change unless they want to. You can't force someone to stop using their phone just as you can't force someone to stop smoking cigarettes or drinking alcohol. We need to look at this issue through an individual lens because we are the only ones who can solve our addiction.

CHAPTER 1

Addiction

Addiction is defined as not having control over doing, taking, or using something to the point where it could be harmful to you.[1] Pay attention to "not having control over doing, taking, or using something," and consider these questions: What's the first thing you do when you wake up? When was the last time you went somewhere without your phone? Do you find yourself checking your phone for no reason? Have you ever gone a whole day without checking your phone? I am guessing as you answered those questions it wasn't what you wanted to hear.

Now, think about how we use our phones throughout the day. When we travel to school or work, public transportation is filled with people glued to their phones, showing no acknowledgment of those around them. Once we get to school or work, students and workers cannot stay off their phones. Next time you are in class, or anywhere, pay attention to how often people check their phones, it is surprising and unsettling. Finally, when we come home, we scroll until we fall asleep with the device in our hand. I don't need to hammer you with statistics to convince you that phone addiction is a real problem because you are already aware of it. The problem is that nobody is taking it seriously, and those who are, do not fully comprehend the issue.

While I won't hammer you with statistics, some can be helpful. I believe phone addiction is the most widespread addiction in history. Currently, ninety-seven percent of American adults and ninety-five percent of American teenagers own a cell phone.[2,3] An official statistic isn't available, but let's lowball an estimate and say half of the phone using population aged fifteen to sixty-five are addicted to their phones (though the true figure is certainly higher). In the US alone that's over 103 million people who are addicted.[4,5] In comparison, in the US around seventy-five million are addicted to alcohol, nicotine, marijuana, opioids, inhalants, cocaine, heroin, stimulants, benzodiazepines, and barbiturates combined (the top ten most common drug addictions).[6] So, even by the most conservative estimate, twenty-eight million more people are addicted to their phones than to the ten most addictive substances in the world combined, and that's just in the United States.

Still, the world treats it as an afterthought. We all want to get off our phones, but we don't see this issue in the same light as addictive substances. Drug addiction is given significant funding and constant attention, and rightly so, but phone addiction is not. When someone has a serious drug problem, they can go into rehab and attempt to recover, but there is no rehab for phone dependency. I can understand why being addicted to our phones cannot kill us like a drug can, but phones and social media take our lives away in a different way. They take away our happiness by forcing us to constantly compare ourselves to others, take away our relationships by making us more concerned with phones than with people, and take away our intelligence by forcing us into echo chambers on social media. Phones won't kill us, but they kill the parts of our lives that truly matter.

Those who are taking this problem seriously and leading the conversation are from generations that did not grow up with this problem. Jonathan Haidt (*Anxious Generation*), Johann Harri (*Stolen Focus*), and Nir Eyal (*Indistractable*) all wrote fantastic books that influenced my writing. Yet, because of their ages, 60, 45, and 44 respectively, they were unable to comment on some nuances at the heart of the phone use and addiction problem. First, they were unable to explain the specific harms that come with how young people use a phone. Bringing attention to these specific harms is important because we are the age group that has been affected by this issue the most. These authors can read about how phones are affecting us, but they will never understand what it's like to be a high schooler and scroll through hundreds of videos on social media of other people having fun, check the Snapchat map to see where people are hanging out, or see a kid they only know from social media and act like they don't know him. To effectively explain the harms of phone usage, these types of experiences need to be highlighted; however, in all of these books, they went unrecognized.

Second, their phone addiction is fundamentally different than younger generations due to the age of first use. It is known that the younger the first use of an addictive substance, the more susceptible someone is to addiction. For example, 95 percent of those who are daily smokers had their first cigarette by the time they were twenty-one.[7] My generation was twelve years old when they first started using a phone, but those who are fifty years old (the average of Haidt's, Hari's and Eyal's ages in 2024) were already thirty-five by the time the first iPhone was released.

These authors undoubtedly have valuable points, but their knowledge of phone addiction is fundamentally different from that of someone who first started using a smartphone in their early teens. While cigarettes have been around for centuries, the iPhone was created less than twenty years ago. Older generations can write about cigarette addiction and connect to younger people as both of their first use of the addictive product could have been at a young age, resulting in the same addictive chemical wiring. However, there is a huge disconnect in how older and younger generations experience phone addiction because each generation's first use occurred at drastically different ages due to the time at which the device was invented. The people who know the most about phone use and addiction are those who are the most vulnerable to phone addiction, grew up using phones every day, and have been affected by it the most—not those who started using them after thirty and can't understand the experiences that truly make phone usage so harmful.

I'm not one of those people skeptical of any change who preach that modern technology will ruin the world. Radio and television were supposed to be the technologies that would ruin society, and now AI is gathering these same claims. Obviously, radio and television didn't ruin our society, so why is the mobile phone different? I believe the phone problem is unprecedented because of two things: power and mobility. Before, we had technologies that could only perform one task. Our TV allowed us to watch shows, our consoles allowed us to play games, and our home phones allowed us to communicate with others. Now, the phone allows us to do all those things on a single device. A phone is so powerful that if we wanted to, we could operate our entire life through it.

The second dimension of the phone problem is mobility. Before phones there were computers that allowed us to do several things, but we couldn't carry computers in our pocket. Smartphones give us the ability to do anything at any time. These two dimensions—power and mobility—are why the phone issue is different. It is just as powerful as the rest of our technologies combined, and it fits in our pocket. This creates a world where we are choosing to use our phones over interacting with the real world.

The final part of phone addiction is the path to quitting. Our phone is intertwined with every part of our lives now: it allows us to communicate and form relationships, get from point A to point B, and even purchase items through mobile credit cards. This makes quitting extremely difficult because we are forced to use our phones every day. However, do not get discouraged; reducing our reliance is a possibility, and I will give you the tools to do so in later chapters.

CHAPTER 2

Why You Should Put Down Your Phone

I think most of us can agree that phone addiction is a real issue, but why does being addicted to our phone matter? I mean we are just scrolling on a device when we are bored. It can't be having that big of an impact, right? In this chapter I want to highlight all the ways you can improve your life by just using your phone less.

Save time

When doing research for this book, I wanted to find out the average screen time for teenagers, but I couldn't find any credible statistics online. The statistics were from unreliable sources or produced by organizations like Common Sense Media, a group that aims to make parents more conscious of how their kids are using their devices. Their screen time average statistic came from the children of these parents, who were already conscious about technology and had created boundaries for their children. This resulted in a skewed representation of the average screen time. It seemed that all of the statistics I found online were not characteristic of the usage I witnessed around me.

So, I conducted my own survey of people aged thirteen to twenty-three from my middle school, high school, and university, obtaining more than 250 responses. Based on my findings, the average phone screen time is five hours and thirty-two minutes per day among this age group. Let's contextualize that number further. First, the recommended amount of sleep for thirteen to eighteen-year-olds is eight to ten hours per night, and it's seven hours for adults.[8] I took the average of the lower end of both statistics because I know most people aren't getting the amount of sleep they are supposed to every night, and I ended up with the assumption that this age group slept an average of 7.5 hours a night. By this measure, adolescents and adults spend more than thirty-three percent of their waking hours on their phone. That is not even including the time they spend on their computers, video game consoles, or watching television.

Now, let's extrapolate those numbers over a lifetime, using the average life expectancy of 77.28 years in the United States,[9] and assume this group uses their phones from age twelve until they die with this average screen time. I picked twelve because this was the age I received my mobile phone and the age at which over seventy percent of children already have a cell phone.[10] Using these assumptions, this group will end up spending 131,844 hours or 5,493 days or **15.05 years** on their phone. That's over fifteen years spent sending messages, scrolling on Instagram, and watching TikTok. There are many ways to put that figure into context, but I like these two: imagine starting your life at fifteen, the year you start your sophomore year of high school, or living to sixty-two instead of seventy-seven.

Let us see how much time we could gain back if we limited our phone use. If this group could lower their screen time to three hours a day, they would still be spending a little over eight years of their lives on their phones, but they'd be getting back almost seven years. If they could cut this further to just an hour a day on their phone, only 2.72 years of their lives would be spent on their phone. You can clearly see the impact. You may think spending only an hour a day on your phone is impossible, but it is the goal we will aim for by the end of this book. As I mentioned in the introduction, this is the time I currently average after I redesigned my phone and changed my habits.

Looking at the amount of time saved on a year-to-year basis is also helpful. By spending only an hour a day on my phone, each year I waste only fifteen days, while my peers who spend five hours and thirty-two minutes a day on their phones waste eighty-four days a year. That means I get to live a 350-day year, while they live a 281-day year. This is a 2.3-month difference you could gain not just this year but every year of your life. Think of the advantages you have with over two more months a year than your peers.

Become more content

When we are constantly forced to compare our experiences to someone else's highlight reel on social media, it is extremely difficult to be content with our life. I remember feeling like my every moment was inadequate, especially when I was bored. During my drive to school, I would see a video of someone else having a great time with their friends, and feel like I was missing out. When I was at lunch I would see photos of men with super attractive women, and wondered why I didn't have a girlfriend, let alone one that looked like Margot Robbie. At home, I would be sitting on the couch watching TV, comfortable with my own situation, and then see posts of families on expensive vacations and wished I was there.

When I was having some success in my own life, social media still found a way to make me less than. After playing well in a basketball game, I would scroll on Instagram and be suffocated with videos of players hitting every single shot they took. I wondered why I couldn't play like them. After dating a girl for the first time, I would see someone else post a romantic photo and worry that my relationship wasn't as secure. As I got older, and became more confident in my appearance, I would see men my age who seemed to be better-looking and have their life figured out. It made me feel like I was falling behind.

Finally, even when I was having the same (or even better) experiences as other people, I still felt like my life was inferior. I would go to the same parties, have a great time, and then spend the last minutes of my night scrolling through all the videos people posted. Their experiences at the same party seemed to be much more entertaining and enjoyable than mine. It made me question if we were even at the same place that night.

What I didn't understand was that these videos and pictures were only highlights of people's lives, not their actual life experiences. The person who posted at the party could have had the worst night of their life but faked it for ten seconds. The family who posted their vacation could have been going through a divorce but forced their kids to smile for the camera. The couple who posted a romantic photo could have been in a toxic relationship. The basketball player could have missed a hundred shots that game, but only the five he made were on social media. The kids my age who looked great and seemed to have their lives together could have posted the one photo where they looked attractive and presentable. In reality, they might be going through tough times, but I would have no idea. Even if you are conscious that social media is a highlight reel, it is hard to repeatedly remind yourself of this every time you scroll.

The major issue with social media is that no matter how happy we are, we can always be made to feel like our lives are second-class. Whether we realize it or not, by using social media we are actively choosing every day to engage in a game that makes us feel worse about ourselves. By disconnecting from it, we become more content.

The other way phones can disrupt how content we are is through over-stimulation. When we are persistently on our phones it causes every second without them to feel boring. This relationship is similar to drug addiction. When drug addicts are not high everything seems dull because they are so used to being in a heightened state. When we are constantly on our phones then choose to go on a walk or read a book it seems extremely boring because these events aren't accompanied by the stimulation we are used to. Not constantly being on our phone will bring back excitement to more trivial tasks.

Increased confidence

Continuous comparison will cause us to feel discontent and reduce our confidence, but our phones hurt our confidence in other ways too. Self-image is everything on social media, which can make even an attractive person feel ugly. As famous model Cameron Russell said, "I'm insecure because I have to think about what I look like every day."[11] She has no reason to be insecure, but she is because she's thinking about what she looks like all the time, similar to how we think and feel when we engage with social media. We are thinking about how we look in our posts and how our posts agree with how we want to be presented to the world. Social media forces us to create a brand for ourselves and maintain it every day. It is exhausting. Most of us do not look like supermodels, so of course perpetual awareness of our image is going to make us feel insecure.

Something else that goes unnoticed is the amount of time we spend looking at ourselves on our phones. Most teenagers use Snapchat and send Snapchats all the time, which forces us to become conscious of how we look. Older generations only became aware of how they looked when they walked past mirrors, but we are reminded of how we look every time we send a Snapchat, which for most of us is about

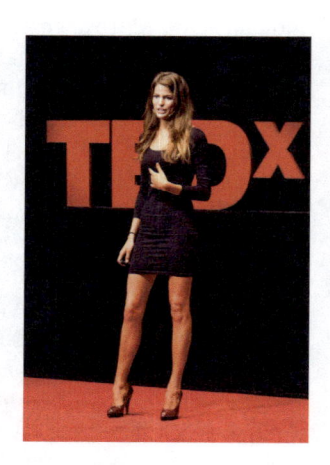

Obviously, Cameron has no reason to feel insecure, but constant thoughts of her appearance forces her to be.

every five to ten minutes. I would recommend we stop looking at ourselves in the Snapchat camera and putting too much emphasis on images. When we look at ourselves in a mirror, photo, or Snapchat camera, it is one angle of millions; not every one of them is going to be our cup of tea. Constantly focusing on our appearance won't alter how others perceive us, and it only make us more insecure.

Become less anxious

During my heavy phone usage days, I always felt anxious. The constant stream of news made me feel like the world was ending, and round-the-clock notifications made me feel like I always needed to respond to something or someone. Social media also made me feel anxious. It felt as if my life was behind others', and I was struggling to "keep up." I was always on edge, and it got to the point where my anxiety was interfering with my everyday life.

When we don't feel like we have something to do at all times, and aren't measuring our life against others, we are going to feel less anxious. It's hard for me to put into words how much my anxiety has decreased and conversely, how much my life satisfaction has improved. When I wrote, "it almost feels like I am living in a completely different world," I was referring to the decrease in my level of anxiety.

Become a better student

The first semester of my freshman year of college was very difficult for me academically. I found it hard to pay attention in class and do my homework because I was constantly drawn to my phone. I remember being unable to stay focused for more than five minutes at a time without being distracted. This resulted in my first semester GPA being dramatically below my intended goal, while taking some of the easiest introductory courses offered at my university. I almost failed an economics test and although I thought I was studying hard, I fell below the average for every single exam in my psychology class. My second semester of my freshman year, when I started improving my relationship with my phone, I was able to significantly improve my GPA. After my freshman year, I continued to decrease my phone addiction and reduced my usage to an hour a day. I was ready to attempt school work without having my phone control my life.

I approached my sophomore year without feeling addicted to my phone, and I instantly saw the changes reflected in my academics. I achieved a 4.0

GPA in both semesters, while taking more credits and tougher courses than during my freshman year. At the same time, I felt less stressed and grasped material faster, even though it was supposed to be more difficult. This is not to say that using my phone less was the only reason my grades improved. I also adopted better study habits and spent more time on my schoolwork, but by putting my phone down, I had so much more time and focus.

The message to take away is that more time and less distraction will lead to better academic outcomes. I remember when I was younger, I thought I was unable to achieve better grades because I just hadn't been afforded the intellectual genetics of a "4.0 student." I thought achieving good grades was only possible for someone like Matt Damon's character from *Good Will Hunting*. This notion, that success in academics is reserved for the chosen few, cannot be further from the truth. Knowledge of a subject is the result of time and effort spent grasping ideas, not genetic predispositions.

The smartest people in history did not create life-changing theories without time and focus. For example, while Albert Einstein is likely naturally smarter than most of us, he wasn't born with any scientific knowledge. He had to read books and conduct thousands of experiments to create groundbreaking theories. It's not like he woke up one day and magically knew that E equals mc squared. Like Einstein, we weren't born with any innate knowledge of history, algebra, or how to read or write. If we want to understand topics, we need time and focus to comprehend them.

Using our phones less gives us this time and focus, offering us the opportunity to understand subjects better and perform well in our classes. When we have more time to study and can use that time more efficiently when not distracted by our phones, we are going to achieve better grades. This advantage especially comes into play when classes are graded on a curve. Even if the student next to us is naturally smarter, we now have an extra four hours and thirty-two minutes that can be used more productively. It becomes extremely difficult for even the "smartest" student to compete with someone who has so much more time and focus.

Even if you are in the workforce, this section still applies to you. Think of the advantages you have when you are more productive and focused than your peers. When you are looking for that next job promotion, you will be able to produce more than your co-workers with substantially less time. Wherever we are in life, time and focus will always benefit us.

Besides academics and work, I cannot emphasize how much more intelligent I feel. I can retain information that I couldn't previously, and I feel I have a better understanding of the world. When I was on my phone all the time, my perspective of the world was a product of a social media algorithm; one that pushed extremist opinions and left out rationality. It made me think the world was going insane. Now my understanding of the world comes through conversations with real people and books, instead of extremist ideologies. Besides being off social media, I also feel more intelligent because I use the newfound time in my life to research things I am interested in. I spend time reading books, or writing this one, instead of watching TikToks. We are more knowledgeable about a subject when we learn about it through a book rather than fifteen-second clips littered with false information. Using our phones less not only makes us better students but can also shape us into more intelligent human beings.

Improve your relationships

I am in such a better mood since putting down my phone, and I find myself wanting to talk to friends and family instead of choosing to scroll on my phone. When I came home from a "long day" during high school, my parents always wanted to talk to me, as most parents do. I was completely dismissive of them as I was stressed about what I thought were a million things going on in my life. My phone was so stimulating and overwhelming that I felt I didn't even have the time to speak to my own parents. It honestly made me a bad son at times. As I have changed my habits, I don't feel the need to constantly check my phone and I have the time to talk to my parents, which I am sure they appreciate.

My relationships with my friends have also greatly improved. When I used social media, every time I took a break in a conversation to check my phone, I was overwhelmed by videos of people who seemed to be closer to their friends and were having more fun that I was. It made me worry that my relationships weren't as strong as other peoples' were. This made me feel the need to prove that my relationships were secure on social media, leading me to post about "great" experiences at the expense of enjoying time with my friends. Now, I am more concerned with the people in my relationships than comparing them.

Improve your social skills

Phone usage gradually weakens our social skills, and every day I believe we are becoming more socially inept. First, our phones have removed our ability to be comfortable with being uncomfortable, which is related to our ability to socialize. When in a social situation, it is a given that we are going to have some moments where we are not speaking to anyone and feel slightly uncomfortable or awkward. Everyone has felt socially anxious before and that is ok and completely normal. However, what's killing our social skills is not us feeling anxious, but our inability to deal with anxious emotions. Instead of being ok with these emotions, we instantly grab our phone to avoid them. We use our phones because they offer us something to do, temporarily removing our feelings of awkwardness and anxiety. You have probably seen memes that make fun of people for scrolling through the weather app when they feel socially anxious. While these posts are made in a comedic tone, their widespread relatability illustrates the decline of our social skills. I encourage you to attempt to notice when people check their phones in a social situation. It almost always happens when someone is feeling anxious or out of place. Paying attention to when people use their phones will also show you how often we use our phones as a social crutch, and will likely deter you from doing so in the future.

Besides giving us a stimulus to remove our feelings of discomfort, our phone also removes these feelings by allowing us to signal to others we are not alone. Texting someone or checking updates allows us to communicate "I am talking to my other friends right now and dealing with important things; I'm not a weirdo who has nobody to talk to." While avoiding the uncomfortable situation is obviously natural, we can see how this is not healthy. If we cannot tolerate being uncomfortable for even a second, our life is going to be very difficult.

Obviously, nobody wants to feel socially anxious, even for a second, and my encouragement to sit with these feelings may seem odd, but if we sit with this discomfort for just a second, it makes all the difference. Using our phones puts us in a never-ending cycle: we go on our phones because we aren't speaking to anyone, and then no one talks to us because we are on our phone. Sitting in silence for just a moment and then making the effort to talk to someone else will break this cycle. Every time I felt uncomfortable between the ages of twelve and nineteen, I used my phone as an escape. As a result, I felt very anxious whenever I wasn't stimulated at a social event. These small moments eventually led me to believe I had some sort of social anxiety. This is a perfect example of how being addicted to our phone can develop into a bigger issue. Now I rarely feel anxious in social situations, and even when I do, I feel better when I see everyone else frantically checking their phones to avoid their own feelings of anxiety.

Second, phones have given us the ability to avoid socializing in person. We have our friends and fellow human beings right next to us, but instead of engaging with them, we choose to be stimulated by our phones. While small interactions may seem insignificant, engaging with a new person broadens our experience of life, and every time we use our phone, we lose that potential opportunity.

Third, social media has harmed us when we are in conversation. One thing that makes someone great at interpersonal interactions is their ability to genuinely care and ask about other people, and social media diminishes this ability. How are we supposed to genuinely care when social media allows us to know everything about everyone? In-person conversations can seem redundant because we already know the answer to every question we might ask.

We have all been in a situation before where we knew what somebody has been up to even though we barely know them. First, I always felt like a stalker: I knew where a girl went to vacation, exactly what she did every day, and had only followed her on Instagram before the conversation. Second, I felt disengaged from conversations. Again, since I knew every answer to every question, I just couldn't be as genuinely interested as I wanted to be. Now, when I am out and haven't seen people for a long time, I get to genuinely learn about what they have been doing, and for people I haven't met, I get to meet them as themselves instead of being influenced by how their Instagram portrays them.

It feels great to not be constantly updated with the news

During my middle school and high school years, I could have recited every single NFL and NBA transaction of the previous hour at any time because of how often I was refreshing Twitter/X and Instagram. While that was cool, I didn't need to know all of that information instantly. Whatever we love learning about in the news, whether it be politics, sports, or something else, we don't need to know what is happening every second despite what today's twenty-four hour news cycle would have us believe.

As many of us know, the "news" includes a lot of excess nonsense. Whether it is overanalyzing who an NFL wide receiver follows on Instagram or what Kanye had for breakfast, this information is inconsequential to our own lives. I don't believe humans are supposed to know everything that is happening in the world every minute of the day. At our roots, we are a species that can only see a finite distance in front of us; we weren't built to perpetually know what is happening everywhere. It is normal and okay for us to be unaware of what is occurring on the other side of the world.

Disengaging from this constant news stream and concentrating instead on our immediate environment is a super rewarding experience. Being disconnected reminds us of how small we are in the grand scheme of things and can relieve the stress of feeling like we always have to meet certain expectations from the wider world. I'm not suggesting we turn a blind eye to horrible events, but we don't need to know about everything that has happened in every millisecond to the seven billion people on our planet. Almost all of what happens to others is out of our control, so we shouldn't spend all of our time worrying about it.

The other problem with the consumption of news these days is that we are fed one article after the next, or one tweet after another, sucking us down a rabbit hole. This style of consumption makes it harder for us to grasp information, and it keeps us scrolling instead of doing something productive.

I feel most of us think the news is biased and/or annoying, but at the same time we cannot completely abandon it. Many of us need the news for work or use it for entertainment. So, I will not recommend we stop our media consumption, but I will recommend we consume it more efficiently. We can do this by listening to podcasts or reading a newspaper once a day instead of endlessly scrolling. There is an option to learn about Congress passing a law at the end of our day instead of at lunchtime or about a sports trade five hours later instead of seconds after the news breaks. The news will be the exact same regardless of when we read it. Consuming news in a more deliberate manner keeps us focused, productive, and happy.

Become less influenced

Continuing on the topic of news, media outlets, both traditional and social, can be echo chambers. When we spend every moment reading news we are going to become influenced, but social media influences us even more than traditional sources. Whether we have liberal or conservative views, on social media we are likely to be pushed an agenda that agrees with our views because the apps want to keep us scrolling as long as possible, it is how they make money. If we are a left-leaning person, we are less likely to be exposed to conservative media because the algorithm knows that we aren't as interested in it.

This algorithm is impactful not only because it puts us in echo chambers but also because it constantly presents fake news. While real news is forced to be bounded in reality, fake news can be stretched to any horizon making it more exciting and more likely to be pushed on social media. It makes sense that according to an MIT study, misinformation spreads six times faster on social media than truthful information.[12]

With traditional media sources, while still potentially biased, there is an opportunity for us to see news that we don't agree with, but social media filters out differing opinions to create a news cycle that only confirms our beliefs, even at the expense of the truth.

This is extremely problematic, but let's consider comments as well. I cannot count the number of times I've gone straight to a comments section after watching a YouTube video so I can read what other people thought of it. When I was younger and saw political videos on the internet, I had no idea what people were even debating, so I would use the comments section to read the thoughts of other people who I assumed to be experts. When I saw comments like "Person A is an idiot," with ten thousand likes, I realized that a lot of people though that Person A was stupid. Even if I initially agreed with what Person A had said, after reading the comments my opinion had changed.

What I didn't realize was that the people commenting were not experts but just people typing online. They, like me, probably had no idea what they were talking about. Trust your intuition, and if you are still confused, use reputable news sources, ask an expert, or read a well-researched book. Do not listen to ChickenIdiot8932 in the Instagram comments.

Even today I still find myself heavily influenced even as a more educated adult. I was recently listening to a diss track through a YouTube video reaction. The diss track was quite complex, and I didn't understand all the references, so I used the video to help me understand and formulate my thoughts about the song. I wanted to construct my own opinion, but I couldn't concentrate on what I thought about the beef because comments were always refreshing on the side of the video. It was difficult for me to form my own opinion because I was being overwhelmed by other people's thoughts. I saw comments like, "Drake lost the beef" and instantly felt swayed to that opinion. When we choose to take in other people's opinions before even formulating our own, we live in a world where our ideas are never really ours.

Better sleep and better mornings

Avoiding using our phone before bed leads to better sleep and more productive days. We have all heard this before, but I want to explain this idea in a little more detail. The first way our phone disrupts our sleep is through the blue light it emits. Our phone restrains our production of melatonin, which is vital to our sleep-wake cycle, known as our circadian rhythm.[13] Secondly, it causes us to not feel relaxed before we fall asleep. When we are responding to people, reading news, or being stimulated in some way, we don't give our minds a chance to relax before bed. Our bedtime should be the time in our day when we decompress, but for a lot of us it is a time where we are overwhelmed with information.

Some of you may be rolling your eyes at this recommendation, just as I used to. I literally could not fall asleep without using my phone, and trying to do so was like begging for insomnia that night. However, I promise using this time before bed to relax is better than being harassed by constant notifications and distractions. I cannot emphasize how pleasant it is to be without interruption, and not feel a responsibility to respond to messages or mindlessly scroll before bed. I find it helpful to reserve the last hour of my day to be without electronics, but a more reliable source, The National Sleep Foundation, recommends that we stop using our phone or any type of device thirty minutes before bed.[14]

When we sleep better, it naturally follows that we awake in a better state to attack our day. We shouldn't ruin it by reaching for our phone first thing in the morning, like I did every day from ages twelve to nineteen. As soon as we do, we are instantly thrown into the outside world of expectation and distraction. I remember the first moments of my day being spent checking who did or didn't respond to me and scrolling through every Instagram, Twitter/X, and TikTok post I'd missed while I was asleep. I remember having the initial moments of my day ruined because a girl I liked hadn't responded to me. I was letting the first emotions of the day be driven by something I couldn't control. Nowadays, I don't put as much emphasis on someone responding to me because I am twenty years old, but I don't need to wake up and know everything that happened in the last eight hours either. It is nice to have those initial moments to myself.

After using my phone directly after waking up, I would check it between showering, brushing my teeth, putting on clothes, and whatever other tasks I had to do in the morning. It was impossible for me to perform my morning routine quickly, as I needed to check my phone between every single task. Doing this always made me feel like I was in a rush, and it felt like I could never start my day off on the right foot. Now, I am able to wake up, do whatever I need to do, and even have a conversation with my parents or roommates without feeling anxious and rushed in the mornings. Giving ourselves restful nights and peaceful mornings allows us to live a more content and productive life.

Live a less self-centered life

Phones curate the larger world into an experience that only a specific individual would enjoy. Our access to news is being filtered so that we are shown only the stories we want to see. Our messages come from friends that only we would understand. Every little bell and whistle conveys that something or someone cares about us or needs our attention.

Past generations had to settle for the limited content available via television, books, or newspapers. Our grandparents never thought of it as "their" TV show or "their" newspaper because it wasn't theirs. It was for the wider public, not specific individuals. Now our entertainment accounts are "ours" because they are completely unique to us, as they only recommend posts or videos that we find interesting. The collection of recommended YouTube videos, the trending section on Netflix, or the order of Instagram posts have all been customized for our specific interests. If someone else accessed these accounts, they would be disinterested.

Spotify emphasizes to users how their listening experience is catered specifically to them.

Being away from our phone allows us take part in a life that isn't all about us. When we read a book, that book wasn't written for us. When we go for a walk, that trail wasn't made for us. When we spend time with our friends and family, those relationships weren't made for only us to be happy. There is give and take between us and others being content. That give and take relationship doesn't exist with our mobile phone. Every moment away from our phone is a moment spent in a more holistic and realistic world.

Become more focused

The advantage of focus is very connected to "become a better student" but it still needs its own section. Before I started to reduce my phone usage, I was unable to sit through TV shows, movies, or anything without checking my phone. I was always thinking about responding to people or checking Instagram. Eventually, I began to prefer simpler movies and TV shows because I literally couldn't understand more complex ones, as they took too much time and attention. Yeah, embarrassing.

Understanding movies and TV shows may seem insignificant, but how we pay attention in other situations certainly is. Previously we talked about how focus can help us study for a test or complete a work assignment, but there are obviously more important things. Like, paying attention to our family or pursuing a passion. I often found myself distracted when listening to the people I cared about or unable to focus on my interests because my addiction to my phone was causing my mind to be elsewhere.

Increased focus gives us the opportunity to take control of our life. We get to do what we set out to do instead of being pulled away by our phone. Luckily, after the changes I made, I can now understand the movie Tenet—just kidding! No amount of time away from a phone will allow anyone to understand that movie.

Be present in your own life

By looking at a text message in class or seeing a party on social media while relaxing at home, we are not engaged in the present moment. We "teleport" ourselves away from what is in front of us. The same is true when posting content or sending messages. When posting, we are thinking about whether our photos are presentable instead of enjoying the moment. When we send messages to friends when we are with others, we engage with the online world instead of being present with the people in front of us. We may not always be witnessing the most interesting thing in the world, but if our mind is continually elsewhere, then we never get to experience and be grateful for what is actually happening.

Improve your emotional intelligence

When we are not stimulated by our phone, we are forced to sit alone with ourselves. When I was on my phone all the time, I couldn't even determine what I was thinking or how I felt because I was always distracted. Using my phone less gave me time to be with myself instead of with Instagram posts of people I didn't know. I now understand my emotions better because I have time without stimulation, which allows me to reflect. At first, it's hard and sometimes scary to have this time to self reflect, but gradually it helps us to become more in tune with ourselves and our emotions. Finding time to not be stimulated is so important and I promise it will help us feel more relaxed over time.

Besides general stimulation and emotional intelligence, social media degrades our ability to be empathetic. It's hard to feel bad for people when we only know the best moments of their lives. After seeing someone win a state championship or graduate from Harvard, how can we feel bad for them? It seems like they are on top of the world. What we aren't seeing is the low moments of their lives, which could be worse than ours, but we would never know. It's hard to be empathetic for others when everyone's life seems not only better than ours, but absolutely perfect.

The empathy disconnection is also prevalent in politics, mostly driven by social media. When we are put in these echo chambers by social media algorithms, we only experience the other side through extremes, which leads us to think the other side is insane. When a Republican-leaning person sees a video online calling for the eradication of white people, they aren't going to have any patience for Democrats. When a Democrat sees a video online of a far-right person praising white power, they are going think all Republicans are crazy. No one is going to have empathy for the opposing side if they are led to believe they are irredeemable. By taking ourselves out of these political bubbles, we get to experience real people who, I promise, aren't as crazy as those we see online.

Divide your life

Before the arrival of smartphones, we only had access to work and school emails when we were at school or the office. Now, work and school follows everyone everywhere. People receive work emails when they are spending time with their families, and students receive assignment reminders and grade notifications while relaxing with friends. Our time with friends and family is time for us, but our phones make us feel like we are constantly on the clock. There is no reason anyone should be checking what assignment they have due or their grades on a Saturday night. When we use our phone for only specific parts of our life, we get the opportunity to channel our life more efficiently, which allows us to become more relaxed.

Conclusion

As you can see, using our phone less will improve our life in so many ways. We gain over fifteen years of our life back; become more content, more confident, less anxious, more intelligent, more successful, more productive, more focused, less influenced, have better relationships, become present in the moment, improve our social skills, have better sleep, have more productive days, and be in tune with ourselves. This issue is so much bigger than just scrolling when we are bored. Using our phone less significantly improves the quality of our lives.

CHAPTER 3

The Social Media Business Model

We have all heard that social media is bad for us, but I always shrugged it off because it was perpetuated by people who didn't understand how it was used. I remember parents around me were forever suspicious of Snapchat. They told me it was only used by criminals who wished to take advantage of the disappearing messages feature to "cover their tracks." I never read or saw anything that could adequately describe a teenager's use of social media.

I wish to provide a refreshing perspective on social media from someone who used these apps every day of his life for seven years, understands how they operate, and can explain firsthand why they are so harmful. But prior to that, it is important to understand how social media is monetized.

The business model

As we all know, social media is free, so how do the corporations that own them make so much money? I remember hearing that it was by taking our data, and I always thought, *"Why would I care? I am not doing anything illegal."* I assume you aren't doing anything illegal either, so why should big tech's collection of our data matter? It's not because they are planning to air our darkest secrets, instead they use it to sell us products and services. These companies have used data to revolutionize the world of marketing forever.

When it comes to marketing, understanding the target market is paramount. The target market is the group of people that would buy a product. Companies are obsessed with focusing their advertising toward this target market because any money spent on trying to woo anyone outside of it is money wasted. For example, if we were selling men's athletic t-shirts, we wouldn't want to advertise to women or men who don't like working out because they wouldn't want our product. The group we would want to advertise to, our target market, would be men who enjoy physical activity.

Not so long ago, corporations were restricted to billboard advertisements and posters on street corners with no guarantee that their target consumer would see them. Then television came along, and marketing became more specialized. Instead of putting our poster on a street corner and praying that our target consumer would see it, we could advertise on certain networks at certain times when we knew our target was more likely to be watching. Let's say we want to sell toys, which would make our target consumer children ages around five to twelve. We know that this age group commonly watches cartoons on Saturday mornings, so we would choose to air our advertisement at that time on a children's network. This money spent on the TV advertisement would probably garner sales for the company and would do a much better job of exposing our target consumer to the advertisement, but nowhere near the efficiency that social media offers now.

Social media transformed marketing from a calculated chance to surgical precision. Before, companies had to hope consumers would see their advertisements on billboards or a TV commercial and then hope consumers would purchase the product. Now social media algorithms are so precise that they can virtually guarantee finding users who will buy the product. But to make this guarantee a reality, they need a lot of data, and they collect this data through their highly addictive "free" apps.

Social media companies use the data they collect to determine who we are and how this relates to our purchasing decisions. These companies know when we are sad, happy, anxious, or angry. When their algorithm detects we are sad as we scroll through photos of our ex-girlfriend's Instagram—yes, they know who our previous partners are—they know to advertise us something that will make the pain go away.[15] Or when they see we liked a post about our sports team winning a game, they know we are excited and will advertise the team gear to us. While algorithms using our data to advertise specifically to us is alarming, what is more terrifying is their ability to use data to manipulate us. They present us with certain posts in anticipation of advertisements so that we feel more inclined to buy a product. For example, the algorithm can show us a photo of someone muscular before advertising us a supplement so we feel like we aren't strong enough and need the product. Marketing used to be similar to a game of roulette, but now it is more comparable to a twisted form of archery where the archer never misses the bullseye.

Besides precision, social media advertising has also given companies the ability to be within arm's length of a consumer at any time. Billboards and TV advertisements are something we see only during certain parts of our days, but we are always using our phones, and even when we aren't, we can be called back by sound notifications. Social media has given corporations the key to consumers' purchasing decisions and 24/7 exposure, revolutionizing the business world forever.

As companies enhance the addictiveness of their apps and refine their algorithms, they can gather more data that yields increasingly precise information. Then they can use this data to make us feel incomplete and nudge us toward a purchasing decision. So, in layman's terms, the business model of social media relies on making us feel worse about ourselves and keeping us addicted to the app. It's messed up.

Of the ten most valuable companies on the planet, three profit from a direct connection to mobile phones and the collection of data. Apple, Google, and Meta (which owns Facebook and Instagram) are some of the world's most recognizable corporations and are currently the first, fourth, and seventh most valuable respectively. But it's not just these companies that benefit from this business model; every company benefits from advertising directly to their target market. Companies no longer have to hope their target consumers see their products. They now go through social media platforms to find them directly. The specialized marketing that social media offers has increased the value of businesses around the world forever.

Social media revolutionized the global economy, so it isn't going anywhere. Instagram or Twitter aren't going to magically shut down, or reduce the addictiveness of their algorithms because doing so would plummet their value. Politicians aren't going to step in because Apple, Google, and Meta are the cornerstones of the world economy. To limit them or the enhanced advertising they provide for other businesses would cause a worldwide recession. The reality is that phones and social media aren't going anywhere. These companies aren't going to self-regulate and no politician is going to pass a impactful big tech bill that would cause devastating financial impacts. Phones and social media are a permanent part of our lives. The absence of political intervention and the nonexistent chance that social media will be changed to benefit us should reinforce that phone addiction is a problem that can only be solved by you.

And no, the TikTok bill does not count. Before the publishing of this book, the outcome of this case has not been decided, but I will go out on a limb and say I guarantee that TikTok will not be banned in the United States. Again, TikTok does too much for businesses for it to be removed entirely in the US. If I'm wrong, I'll look like an idiot, but I'm willing to take that chance to prove a point.

Why is social media so addictive?

I want to make you aware of the specific tricks that social media companies use to get us hooked. This will help you understand how you are being manipulated, and why we will take the steps we do in later chapters to curb our phone addiction.

Jackpot!

Guaranteeing a new stimulus every time we open our phone is extremely powerful. Social media is similar to a slot machine: every time we pull the lever/open the app, we get something new. We know that whenever we click on Instagram, Twitter/X, or Snapchat, we will be given new updates. As you may have noticed, these companies are continually evolving their platforms to find new ways to overload us with stimulus. Instagram added "stories", Snapchat added "discover stories" (the advertisement/corporate stories), and Twitter/X added talk rooms that are seemingly endless. Now, apps that aren't even related to social media, like the Amazon app, have added social media-like feeds because they are aware it gets users hooked.

Social media companies also copy their competitors when they see them succeed in increasing engagement. One of the first examples was Instagram taking "stories" from Snapchat, but the most prevalent example has been TikTok. TikTok revolutionized the fifteen-second video market, and now every company has their own version of it. Facebook has Reels, Instagram has Instagram Reels, and YouTube has YouTube Shorts. Everyone in the industry has followed suit because they recognized more stimulus makes their apps more addictive and, thus, more profitable.

Your feed is tailored for you

Every single person's feed is created specifically for them. Previously, we touched on how content is filtered differently based on what keeps us most engaged. I receive sports content and photos of my friends on social media, while my mother sees Pilates videos.

Besides differences in content, posts are not ordered chronologically but in an order that is most likely to prolong our engagement on the app. To test this hypothesis, go on a friend's Instagram feed and compare it to yours. You are likely to follow some of the same people, have similar interests, yet your Instagram stories will be presented in a markedly different order. For example, you may notice that your ex-girlfriend/boyfriend posted ten hours ago, but that post is presented first on your feed. Whereas on your friend's feed the same post may not be shown when they log in. The algorithm knows that your ex's post will keep you engaged the longest and therefore makes it the first thing you see. That is pretty disturbing to me!

Little tricks

All social media companies have little tricks up their sleeves. Features like the bouncing three dots when someone is in the process of direct messaging were created so we think, *I don't want to leave the app; they are about to text me.* Instagram's color scheme and the way it responds to us clicking a message or refreshing our feed was designed to be addictive.

Even when we are not using the app, it has tricks to lure us back in. For example: When we are tagged in a post or comment, the app will alert us so we are incentivized to open it back up. This also happens when we aren't even tagged in a post. We have probably seen notifications like, "James posted for the first time in a while!" This notification and all notifications are tricks designed to get us back on the app to collect more data.

Human psychology

Socializing is innate to the human experience; it is embedded in our DNA. Anything that fosters this can become addictive, especially when companies pair it with techniques like using bright colors and refreshable feeds. Not so long ago, only some social media had direct messaging, but now there is Instagram DM, Facebook DM, TikTok DM, Twitter/X DM, etc. These companies realize the more connected we feel to our friends, the more we want to be on the app and the harder it is for us to delete them.

Celebrity

The thing that social media does best is tap into our egos. Likes and comments make us feel important, like the entire world cares about us. Imagine you have posted an Instagram photo and gained five hundred likes and sixty-four comments. That's 564 people paying attention to you. Imagine if 564 people in real life were commenting on what you were doing and telling you that they liked you; you would feel like a celebrity. We probably are only good friends with about thirty of the people who liked and commented, so this massive amount of recognition from strangers understandably can make us feel important, appreciated, and famous.

Social media has allowed us all to become celebrities. There now are thousands of "influencers" with millions of followers who a generation ago would never have been noticed. Back then, someone had to be a movie star, professional athlete, or rock star to be a celebrity. Now, anyone can become famous for just unwrapping some toys or playing a video game. We love the fact that every time we post there is a small chance that we, too, could go viral and become famous; it keeps us hooked.

Aside from the larger world, we can still be famous in the microcosm of our communities. I remember during my high school years, there were hundreds of kids who became "celebrities." They became famous because of their attractiveness, funny videos they posted, or some other niche. Obviously, kids have been popular in the past, but how they are famous today is drastically different from social hierarchies of the past. High school "celebrities" used to be constrained by the walls of their school. Now, popular kids are not only known within their school, but by any young person with a phone.

Eventually, as we get older, everyone becomes a "celebrity" in their own right because we all have thousands of followers. We can go places and be recognized or recognize someone else solely because of Instagram. Everyone has had a moment when we saw someone we knew from Instagram but had to act like we didn't know them. In these moments people become like celebrities because they are recognizable without any previous introduction. Before social media we would have never known them, but their Instagram has allowed them to become "famous."

Social media, whether it be in smaller social circles or the larger world, has given everyone the ability to feel important, which may be the most addictive substance ever created. Now everyone can feel like the center of attention, even as they sit scrolling in the corner. To quote the movie *The Incredibles*, "With everyone super, no one will be." In the world of social media, "With everyone a celebrity, no one is." But it doesn't matter to these corporations if the majority of us are not actually famous, as long as we feel admired and remain addicted to their apps.

CHAPTER 4

How Social Media Actually Affects People Today

Our parents' generation still struggles to understand social media. They get that seeing perfect images of people all the time damages our self-esteem, but they are not privy to the intricacies of the platforms. In this chapter, I want to explore exactly how social media is used and why it is so harmful.

Social media and mental health

I could give a thousand statistics about how social media is damaging our mental health (we'll get to that shortly), but I want to take a more personal approach first. We all know what it's like to feel "less than" because of social media. It doesn't take a therapist to know that constantly looking at highly edited photos, taken at the perfect angle, of beautiful people in exotic locations is going to make us feel bad about ourselves, especially when we are sitting at home doing nothing. When everyone looks happy and perfect, it makes us feel like there is something wrong with our life if it's not all sunshine and rainbows. There is a reason most of the top staff at tech companies do not allow their children to access social media. Facebook's former Vice President of Growth openly admitted this, saying his own kids "aren't allowed to use that shit."[16]

Now for the statistics, since 2009 when social media started to boom on the mobile phone, the number of hospital admissions for nonfatal self-harm is up sixty-two percent for girls ages fifteen to nineteen and 189 percent for girls aged ten to fourteen. In the US, the CDC found that suicides are up seventy percent among girls aged fifteen to nineteen and 151 percent for girls aged ten to fourteen compared to before social media in the 2000s.[17]

Touching on different mental health issues, since 2010 there has been a 161 percent increase in major depressive episodes for boys and a 146 percent increase for girls. A similar pattern emerges for levels of high anxiety among young adults, with a 139 percent increase in the age group eighteen to twenty-five, and a 103 percent increase in age group twenty-six to thirty-four.[18] The doubling of anxiety and suicide rates in these age brackets illuminates how serious this issue is. Never before has there been a mental health crisis this clear.

Regardless of these statistics, we should not have the mentality of a victim. While our mental health has deteriorated because of social media, we are also part of the problem. We are all guilty of only posting the best versions of ourselves on social media. If you looked at my Instagram, you would see my ten best photos. They are not photos of me after I failed in life but after some of my greatest successes, proving that I, too, was contributing to the problem. Yet it's no surprise, given the landscape, that people do not want to post a bad photo of themselves when everyone else is showing off the best version of their life. To do so would make our life appear to be worse in comparison. In truth, we are neither heroes nor villains but rather characters in a story where everyone continues to lose.

Social media and perfection

Social media has created a culture in which whatever gets someone scrolling is praised. People don't want to see an average looking man or woman when they could see a better looking one. A photo of an average motel in Wisconsin is not going to be as interesting as a luxurious hotel in Italy. Social media has created a culture of perfection because this is what drives views and likes.

This culture has caused an inflation in the style of posting. Posting used to be unedited photos of friends hanging out, but now even simple experiences are edited and made to look "perfect." Take a look at this 6-year difference in a post at a concert on social media.

An 18 year old's Instagram photo at a concert in 2017 vs an 18 year old's Instagram photo at a concert in 2023.

Almost every post today is accompanied by a multitude of edits and filters to fit in with the latest Instagram style. In the post from 2017 we can see ourselves having that experience, but the post from 2023 more closely resembles a movie set than any moment you or I have ever had.

Someone could have made the case ten years ago that social media was a platform to share our lives with our friends and family, but it has evolved past that. It is a bragging contest that only consists of people at their best angles having their best experiences. We can't expect to be happy when the moments we "see" our peers having seem not only extravagant but unlike any experience we could have.

The problem with Snapchat

Most people can understand the harm of apps like Instagram, but aren't able to touch on the nuances of Snapchat, which I believe to be more harmful. For those who don't know, Snapchat serves as most teenagers' primary form of communication. Standard messaging apps are used but not as often because, frankly, they are not as stimulating as Snapchat. Snapchat offers photos, videos, texts, streaks, a live location map of your friends, and the "stories" feature, which all keep users more engaged than normal texting apps.

Snapchat "stories" are the heart of the platform and are similar to Instagram posts but only "friends" (you aren't necessarily friends with people on Snapchat as they are just people you know) can see them and they only are viewable for twenty-four hours. There are two types of "stories" your friends can post: public and private. "Public Stories" go out to all friends, while "private stories" go out to a select group of friends. To be honest, though, "private stories" are not very private and frequently have upwards of two hundred selected people on them.

What makes Snapchat so harmful, and what separates it from Instagram, is frequency. People post on their Snapchat stories constantly. People post things like what they are eating and who they are hanging out with. "Stories" are not thought of as being as important as Instagram posts but are still very curated. Think of it like this: Instagram posts are the highlighted versions of people's triumphs, while Snapchat stories are the highlights of people's every second.

Snapchat's frequency of posts makes you feel as if your every moment is inadequate. Every single second of people's lives, from how they joke with their friends, eat dinner with their families, or how they choose to relax, is documented in an exaggerated fashion. We know that we probably won't win the state championship or drive a Ferrari, but feeling like how we hang out with our friends is less than or how we interact with our families is unorthodox, is a whole new level of insecurity that none of us asked for.

In addition to constantly making me feel less than, Snapchat always made me feel alone. I cannot count the number of times I was sitting at home, comfortable in my own situation, and then saw other people hanging out in a "story." Even if I was with friends earlier that day, it made me feel like I was missing out on something. A friend told me, "I feel like Snapchat makes me have this constant pressure to go out and hang out with people; it is what feels normal. I go out not because I love to but because it is what everyone else seems to be doing. I would rather go out and feel normal than sit at home alone and feel weird." Whether you already understand the harm of "stories," or this concept is entirely new to you, you can see the problem. However, Snapchat's stories feature is only the tip of the iceberg.

Snapchat is so invasive that at times I wonder how it is even legal. Its location map feature allows users to see where other users are in the world and how long ago they were logged into the app. The first thought that comes to mind is that a stalker could use this information to potentially kidnap or, worse, kill somebody. An earlier version of Snapchat+, Snapchat's subscription service, made it even easier for a potential stalker to track someone. It enabled you to see a "friend's" movement on the map throughout the day. So you could see the exact streets Jimmy took from his house to his job downtown, and the exact time he came home. Through Snapchat+, anyone could easily map out a person's entire schedule—not just what they did throughout the day but exactly where they were and when they did it. Let that sink in for a second. That is terrifying.

Hopefully, most of us aren't stalkers or serial killers, so what are the everyday effects of this function? People frequently scroll to the location map to see where their "friends" are. I remember looking at the map and seeing twenty of my "friends" pop up at a popular spot or house party. I would feel left out even if I didn't know anyone there. The other layer to this is that teens commonly will only turn on their location when they are out to showcase they are at a cool event. Even when people aren't actively posting, they are still trying to showcase the best versions of themselves.

Just as we don't need the news to tell us what is happening everywhere all the time, we don't need to know what someone else is doing every minute of the day. Only after breaking my addiction to my phone can I say I'm completely comfortable staying in, and I only feel this way because I no longer expose myself to a barrage of social media comparison.

The overall problem with Snapchat, whether it be "stories" or the live location map, is that it forces us to compare our every second to someone else's best moment. This is clearly no way to live. I realized that, since the age of twelve, the day I downloaded Snapchat, I compared every second of my life to that of an "ideal" human being. No wonder I wasn't happy.

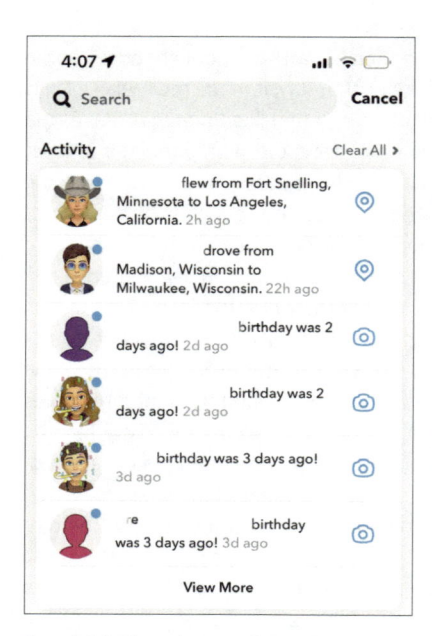

Snapchat displays where people have traveled to and from, how long ago a user was using the app, where they were located, and what they were doing. In this case, the user that was using the app when I was logged into Snapchat was listening to music.

36 Enemy in Your Pocket

Finally, Snapchat's problems are exacerbated by the difficulty of deleting it. When Snapchat is our primary form of communication, deleting it is almost impossible. Getting rid of it would be a decision to lose relationships. So, in Chapter 7, "Redesign Your Phone," instead of deleting Snapchat, we will take steps to reconfigure our Snapchat to remove the harmful parts but preserve the communication element.

Knowing too much

Many argue that the greatest benefit of smartphones is access to information. People can now educate themselves through online courses such as those provided by Khan Academy, and Twitter/X gives us the inside scoop on politics and sports. The mobile phone has allowed the average human to know more than ever before.

At the same time, this abundance of information has repercussions. Social media gives us a creepy amount of knowledge about people we have never met. I would know a kid in my class got into an argument with his parents at 8:00 p.m. on a Tuesday because of a Snapchat private story. I would know a girl from Tennessee, through a friend of a friend, just broke up with her boyfriend because of a close friend's Instagram story. I would see where my friend's ex-girlfriend from sixth grade was on a Wednesday night because of the Snapchat map. When my phone usage was at its peak, I knew so much about others' friendships, beefs, and break-ups, without even attempting to stalk people. It felt invasive.

I remember once seeing an Instagram story from an acquaintance and her friends on a boat. As I was going home, I noticed one of the guys from the story walking back from the boat and thought, *I know exactly what you did today, but you have no idea who I am.* Just weird!

Your social media "community"

Our social media community consists of all the followers and "friends" on our accounts that don't have an impact on our life. Many of us have hundreds, maybe even thousands of followers, but that doesn't mean we are friends with those people in real life. This fake community doesn't really exist, but we still subject ourselves to all of these people's lives by following them. It causes us to be concerned about the opinion of people we have only seen on social media. I know all of us had an entire community of people from other high schools when we were younger that we only knew through social media.

Our social media community grows over time as we transition to different stages of our lives and still follow the people we knew from middle school, high school, and college. We continuously build a bigger community of people who no longer have an impact on our lives. Ella from high school might not be a part of our lives in any way, shape, or form, but it feels like she still is when we log in every day and see her.

I enjoy the way the famous singer-songwriter Mac DeMarco articulates this point: "It is an illusion that they are still a part of my life."[19] He is talking about seeing a post from someone he barely knew in high school and has no connection to now. That person only exists to him on social media, not in real life, so he doesn't need to spend any time thinking about them.

Social media and branding

Our social media represents how we want to be seen by the world; it is the brand we have created. Instagram and Snapchat represent how we want to present ourselves socially, while LinkedIn shows our professional persona. On every social media platform, we work as our own brand manager to portray our best image. When we post a photo, we first want to make sure we look good, but we also are concerned with what the image says about us. When we post a photo at a party, the message is, "I am cool and have friends." When we post an image of us relaxing on the grass with a book the message is, "I am a peaceful person." When we post a photo at an expensive resort, the message is "I am wealthy." Whatever the photo is, it has an underlying message that is part of the brand we portray on the internet whether we are conscious of this or not.

At any moment we can search somebody's brand. Essentially, an advertisement is running every second of every day for our entire lives. After meeting someone it is a pretty common practice afterward to follow them on Instagram. We already met them in person, but now we can judge them by how they choose to present themselves online and then reevaluate them.

This happens with not only people you know but also those you don't. I have had buddies say to me, "You know this guy?" I then look up his Instagram to see his posts. If he posts something with his family, I assume he's a put together guy, but if he posts himself obviously blackout drunk, I assume he's a degenerate. I have never met this person, but I already have assumed so much about him based on his social media brand. Also, when people's accounts are often just their names that is all we need to see the entire brand they have cultivated for themselves.

Some may think that this brand is only important to who you are online, but it also bleeds into the real world. In college, I know that within clubs, intramural sports, or fraternities and sororities, your Instagram presentation matters in terms of your inclusion in that club or group. I have heard statements like, "He was cool, but his Instagram is just really weird, man," and "There is no way she posted that; she has to be off." Your brand on social media is extremely important to social success online but also matters to how you are perceived in the real world.

Some of the data included in the analysis of a "good" social media brand is your following "ratio" and the amount of likes you get. "Ratio" refers to the idea that it is better to have more followers than people you are following. You calculate your "ratio" by dividing the number of followers by the number of people you're following. Your goal is to have a ratio above one, denoting that your followers number is larger than your following number. This was an obsession for me and other kids when I was in high school. I remember people following me, so I would follow them back, just for them to unfollow me a day later, so they could increase their "ratio." It should be noted, this situation actually unearthed two losers, the person that unfollowed me, and myself, as I was actively tracking the number of followers I had.

"Ratio" itself is not a powerful enough statistic to prove your worth, as likes are also very important. If you have a great "ratio" but not enough likes, it signifies your followers are not active or are fake (people commonly buy followers). I once said to a friend, "You may have a better ratio than me, but my 'like' ratio is way better than yours," and yes, I was serious.

While "ratio" and likes showcase how branding on social media has become so important, it is still an oversimplification of the issue. Yes, it is desirable to have a better "ratio" or more likes, but you can still get a general vibe of people based on their Instagram regardless of these "statistics." What people post is more important in how you judge them than what their "ratio" or likes say about them.

The problem that exists with branding and social media is that we are constantly acting as marketing managers for ourselves, and that is stupid. We shouldn't always be worrying about an online brand because it is exhausting and anxiety producing. Somebody's Instagram brand is the least representative example of who someone is, as it has conveniently left out all of the awkwardness and failures in one's life.

Social media and sexualization

As I have become older, I have seen a massive increase in sexualization on social media. When I was in middle school my peers were not posting photos of themselves in bikinis, but I remember when someone older than me, like a high schooler, posted a photo of their butt or breasts on Instagram it was a big deal. People would spend days talking about the scandalous photo someone posted.

Nowadays, posting a photo of yourself half naked almost feels like a requirement for young women. Teenage girls post individual photos of just their breasts or butt on Instagram, and nobody bats an eye. Sexualization is such a norm that people notice when women don't post this way, and they start to develop a "prude" reputation. My female friends tell me there is an immense pressure to keep up with this culture and it is exhausting for them.

I don't write this to just shame girls because guys also sexualize themselves. Photos of men flexing in the gym or shirtless on vacation are common practice. Regardless of gender, we all are susceptible to the need to fit in. We are products of our environments, and when the norm is to post in sexualized ways, we follow suit.

Social media and schools of thought

We talked earlier about how social media is more influential then traditional media in terms of news, but it also can negatively form our views on life. Let me give an example: On TikTok, there is a tendency among gym goers to glorify depression. People post about "fighting their demons" like they are heroic loners and encourage others to isolate themselves from their friends to only focus on working out. This type of post came up on my feed all the time on TikTok as a teenage boy, and it was an appealing fantasy to me, as I was young and impressionable. Obviously, this is an idiotic way of viewing life, but so many young men like me continue to engage with it because of its celebration on TikTok.

Young people see this celebration and attempt to act in accordance with it instead of being happy and spending time with friends. This leads to these gym goers feeling depressed, and then once the social media app realizes they like these types of videos, it continues to direct these videos to them, even though it is decreasing their happiness. Social media doesn't just influence our life one time like watching a movie but continuously forms our view of life regardless of what is best for us.

You may be thinking, I *engage with very positive posts about self-improvement, budgeting, books, etc., and engaging with social media improves my life*. You may be engaging with positive information, but consider whether you are acting on the information you are seeing or simply feeding your social media addiction? Are you taking the necessary steps to improve yourself or just using these posts to think you are bettering your life? Regardless, there are more reliable sources and more focused environments in which to absorb this information. Instead of scrolling through social media to find a self-improvement video, read an article, book, or watch a documentary. If we truly care about a topic, this should be easy. If not, this is a tell-tale sign we are more addicted to our phone than we care about gaining knowledge on that subject.

TD Ameritrade ran an advertisement showcasing how we are bombarded on social media with "get-rich-quick" videos. The commercial starts with videos surrounding a person until the videos disappear to show just a few bits of reliable information about wealth management. When the person wasn't overwhelmed with information it allowed them to understand how to improve their financial situation.[20] This is how I want you to approach information that you want to learn about. Choose a more focused and reliable channel rather than listening to a bunch of random users online.

Social media and experiences

I won't reiterate how seeing experiences on social media will cause us to be less content, but I will touch on how even sharing can ruin experiences. Social media forced me to look at experiences through a lens of how I was going to post about them instead of my enjoyment of the experience. Even when I wasn't directly seeing other people's highlighted lives, I was still concerned with making sure my life measured up with theirs. I remember in middle school and high school traveling to specific places just so I could post a photo of myself. For example: I would go to the lakefront so I could post a photo of myself because that was the "cool" place to hang out. I traveled there not because I wanted to have that experience but rather I wanted to be seen doing it. I had become a slave to what I perceived other people wanted to see.

I think it has become hard for my age group to have a great time unless we let other people know that we are having the best experience ever. When we have been accustomed to only seeing photos of perfect families, we want to let other people know that our families are doing great as well. It feels like if we don't post a photo of our happy family, then we must be having problems. Even before social media, people were aware of the effect comparison had on our mental health. Some may be familiar with Theodore Roosevelt's quote, "Comparison is the thief of joy." Roosevelt said this in the nineteenth century; I wonder what he would say today?

Social media and growing up

As we expose children at younger ages to social media, we are robbing them of their innocence earlier in their lives. Children on social media are exposed to older generations and, inevitably, want to copy them. Younger age groups have always looked up to older ones and copied what they do, and I am not recommending that changes. We all wanted to dress and act like high schoolers when we were in middle school, and having role models is beneficial for young kids. But these days, children's role models are random people on the internet, not older kids in their communities.

Kids as young as ten are exposed to how college students and older people are acting and dressing. They no longer see people only a few years older than them as "cool" but adults nearly twice their age. I have seen children as young as eight on social media making sexual jokes in alignment with trends they have seen. The commenters obviously thought it was hilarious, but this eight-year-old was making jokes about things I didn't comprehend until I was seventeen years old. The capability for young children to see how people decades older than them act is resulting in children maturing faster than ever before.

Furthermore, younger children are also becoming sexualized at an earlier age because of social media. When I was on TikTok, almost every dance involved turning around and showing your butt to the camera. Young, impressionable children are obviously inclined to follow these trends. This has created a world where my friends' ten-year-old sisters are actively shaking their butts on TikTok because it is the dance that is "in." If this doesn't wake you up to the problems caused by social media, then I don't know what will.

Social media and hookup culture

Instagram serves a form of validation, a "token" people show to others to prove the attractiveness of their mate. When someone tells their friends about a person they have been seeing, the first words anyone in my generation says are, "Let me see their Instagram." If their partner's Instagram is "attractive," then they receive validation regardless of how they look in person. If their partner is attractive in real life but their Instagram doesn't reflect that, then they receive questioning looks from friends.

Instagram and someone's appearance in real life is so intertwined that if someone's Instagram is "subpar" then their real life reputation of their attractiveness begins to diminish. On the contrary, I have also observed someone's real life reputation of their attractiveness increase due to how they look on Instagram. This issue has become so insane that I have heard statements like, "I don't think she is good looking, but her Instagram is just too attractive."

Social media and relationships

I have always found the performative gestures people make in regard to their relationships on social media odd. It's like people are more concerned with proving they are dating somebody than being in a relationship with that person. For instance, I saw a couple both post a love letter on Instagram for their two-year anniversary. Instead of sending these letters to each other privately, they choose to send them over a public platform to everyone, emphasizing that they wanted to showcase the quality of their relationship to others.

Besides romantic relationships, I also see people posting long, elaborate love letters to each other on social media in a desperate attempt to prove the "quality" of their friendships. I have encountered some very strange odes to friendships such as, "Happy birthday, my Lily. I would be entirely lost without you. My soulmate. I love you more than you will ever know," or "To another decade of Ivy. I have grown up with you in so many ways, you continue to teach me more about myself and the world every day. You and me forever. I love living life with you, magical human." Obviously these captions are extremely odd and performative, but we don't notice because they are the norm on social media. Even if we felt this strongly about someone, why not message them privately instead of being concerned with impressing other people.

Finally, we also see this pattern in familial relationships. I saw posts of people celebrating their parent's birthday or posts about Father's or Mother's Day when I knew their parents didn't have Instagram. In the situations illustrated in the previous paragraphs, you could have made a claim that those posts were a form of affection, but in this situation, you simply can't. When someone's parents can't even see what they are posting, it is only about themselves. It is about them showing how close they are with their family and attempting to impress others with the "great" child-parent relationship they have.

In all of these types of posts, we see a common theme: performance. These photos and captions serve to prove that their relationships are strong and to brag about how close they are to the people in their lives. It's sad that we express our affection for friends, partners, and family by trying to impress random people on the internet, instead of showing our love to them.

Social media and wealth

A smart friend of mine once said, "Social media is a platform for human behavior that would have happened anyway," and I believe this statement is especially accurate when it comes to showcasing wealth. Obviously, ostentatious people exist in real life and are always going to exist, but I wanted to illuminate how this dynamic has evolved on social media.

People used to showcase their wealth by subtly posting a photo of them at an expensive resort. Now, people have skipped the step of including themselves in the photo and now only post the expensive vacation they were able to afford. It's unfortunate because I think many aren't aware of their display of wealth and aren't attempting to post in a malicious way. Rather, they are following a trend of posting what is appealing to the eye. People get more attention when they post a photo of a Jeep instead of a Toyota, or post a photo in Cabo instead of Des Moines. Regardless of people's intentions, the way wealth is being presented on social media is progressively getting nastier.

Instagram photos of hotel rooms and expensive resort locations.

CHAPTER 5

Can We Fix Social Media?

We know that the way social media is being used today causes mental health issues, but could we fix this toxic culture? There have been many attempts to fix social media, and the most recent attempt was the introduction of the app BeReal. It was released in 2020 with the mission of making social media more authentic and less toxic. BeReal attempts to do this by allowing users to post only once a day, when a daily notification is sent out. For example, a notification could be sent out at 12:35 p.m., and when users clicked on it, they had only one minute to take a photo. With a random posting time, and minimal time to prepare, the idea was people would have to post what they were actually doing and how they actually looked. The days of posing and showing only the highlights of your life would be over.

BeReal started small with some dedicated users in their own small social circles unconnected to the larger world. During this time, the photos that came up on my feed were taken at the time of the notification and genuinely showed what people were doing. I saw friends looking casual and doing uneventful things like walking their dogs. But as more and more people downloaded the app and the number of "friends" people had increased, things changed.

First, photos became less genuine. Everyone started to look a lot better and miraculously had more exciting lives. All of a sudden, my feed went from showing people doing homework to people at concerts and parties. Eventually, it became a trend for people to post their coolest BeReals on Instagram.

Second, people found ways to game the system. The timer for BeReal only started when you clicked on the notification. So, you could see the notification at 8:00 a.m., when you looked tired eating cereal but take the photo at 11:30 p.m., when you looked great at a party. It got to the point where it was common to talk about waiting to take your BeReal until you were doing something cool. Everyone knew that everyone else was waiting, so they did the same.

People also gamed the system through the retakes feature, which was part of what made BeReal "real." Retakes showed your friends how many times you retook the photo before posting, which incentivized you to post the first photo you took. If you were caught with multiple retakes, you would be made fun of. Eventually though, people found a way around this too. By swiping out of the app you could restart the retake counter. So, someone could take a hundred photos before posting, but if they refreshed after the ninety-ninth retake, it would show they had no retakes. Eventually, everyone's photos had zero retakes and zero "realness." The app that was meant to fix social media ended up with the same toxic culture. The moral of the story is that social media as a concept may be not be malicious, but it will always foster a culture of only the highlights of individuals' lives, and, consequently harm our mental health.

The transition of BeReal photos over time.

Deleting social media

Given social media's addictiveness, potential for harm, and inability to change, I highly recommend deleting almost all social media accounts, but I know for many that decision is hard. Deleting TikTok and Twitter/X are much easier decisions, as not much direct socializing happens on these platforms and deleting them does not feel like an attempt to delete your social life. You would rarely/never ask a peer to hang out through a TikTok or Twitter/X direct message.

Instagram, Snapchat, and LinkedIn are a completely different story. Our social lives exists on these apps, and it feels like deleting them is an attempt to cut us off from our social worlds. First, LinkedIn feels impossible to delete, as it can be directly connected to professional opportunities, but do not be confused! It suffers from the same effects as other social media. If we have been searching for an job for a year and then see someone our age just got hired by Goldman Sachs, we aren't going to feel great about ourselves. And trust me, nobody is posting about the jobs they weren't hired for or the promotion they didn't receive.

Instagram, on the other hand, I can definitely live without. I no longer need to be concerned with what people from high school are doing or need to post the best photos of myself **to try to impress people who don't even know who I am**. I don't need to, or want to, measure myself constantly against the best version of other people's lives.

I know even after reading this book, the decision to delete Instagram is difficult, as again, it seems it is a decision to delete our social life, but I promise we will still have friends. I want to emphasize again, *Instagram is a make-believe world*. We only lose our connection to this fake world when we delete the app. The people we want to stay in contact with we can choose to stay in contact with. There is no reason we need to scroll through Steve from high school's five-star European vacation on a Tuesday night.

Finally, Snapchat is the last social media platform we need to be concerned with. Deleting Snapchat is extremely difficult, as it is so intertwined with our communication with friends. Again, in the final chapters, we will address this problem by deleting the social media aspects of Snapchat while preserving the communication tools.

CHAPTER 6

The Phone Beyond Social Media

It is easy to scapegoat social media as the sole reason that our phones are harmful, but phones can also hurt us in other ways. Again, we can do virtually everything on our phones, which opens the floodgates for potential harm. To say social media is the only problem would be an oversimplification. Our relationships with messaging, music, porn, gambling, and other apps on our phones also greatly affect our lives.

Messaging and relationships

I have had endless conversations with my friends about how message notifications impact their happiness. Everyone has had to wait endlessly for a text from somebody they like. I had days when I was younger that were made or destroyed by a response or the absence of one. My friends tell me the same thing, "She/he hasn't responded to me in five hours. They must want to break up with me." People fear that if someone hasn't responded quickly enough then they no longer love them. This sounds stupid, but it is a common experience among adolescents nowadays. It gets to the point where teens are constantly refreshing their Snapchat maps to see when the person they like logged on last.

We think there is a connection between the success of our relationships and how often our partner responds. People treat response time as a barometer for how much a person likes them, even when they are already in a relationship with that person. A response time of two hours is supposed to be a sign that someone is disinterested, while a reply in five minutes is supposed to be a be evidence that someone is obsessed with you. We value our relationships based on these response times because we think they serve as a true reflection of someone's affection towards us. We know that everyone is constantly on their phones, so when someone doesn't respond instantly, it feels like a conscious choice to ignore us.

The messaging dilemma, regardless of how childish it sounds, is a significant issue. Responding every second of the day is unsustainable and overwhelming, and in turn this has created relationships with the same characteristics. Younger relationships are now defined by constant attachment because without it many don't feel loved.

Music stimulation

Nowadays, we are always listening to music: between home and school, between school and work, while at the gym, when we get home, and whenever we have the chance. We are either looking at something or listening to something, rarely allowing ourselves to be away from technology. Answer honestly: when's the last time you walked to class/work without headphones? Next time you go somewhere, notice how many people have their headphones on. It feels like we are in an episode of the Netflix series *Black Mirror*.

As a society, we are never giving ourselves a chance to be without stimulation and be present in the moment. When we never give ourselves a second to relax, we are going to be stressed. It may seem crazy to some that listening to music could have a negative effect on our life, as studies have proved it can reduce stress. But, as with anything else, we can have too much of a good thing. Think of it like this: working out is great for us, but if we do it all day, every day, we will start to develop injuries. Similarly, music is enjoyable, but if we are listening to music every second, we never give ourselves a chance to think.

It is also important to be conscious of how music can manipulate our emotions. Music is incredible at influencing how we feel, and when we play music all the time, it can start to affect our mood. Playing one sad song isn't going to cause us to be depressed, but when we fill our ears with sadness throughout the day, it can start to have a significant impact. For example, I really enjoy listening to Zach Bryan, but he creates some really depressing music. I remember being in great moods, then turning on some of his songs and thinking, *why do I feel so sad all of the sudden?* If you notice that your music is bringing you down, try to put on some more upbeat songs. If you are listening to music or podcasts all the time and find yourself stressed, find moments without audio. Give yourself a second to be without any noise or flashing lights. I promise you that you will find yourself in a significantly better mental space.

Gambling

The mobile phone has significantly exacerbated gambling addiction. Before smart-phones, gamblers were forced to go through a lengthier process when placing a bet. They had to think of a game to bet on, drive to a casino, and then walk up to the counter. In this situation, the gambler has many opportunities to rethink their decision. Now, when gambling addicts get the urge to bet, they can pick up their phone and place a bet wherever they are, in a matter of seconds, with just the click of a button. The barriers to placing a bet and thinking through a gambling decision have been completely eliminated. It is no surprise that gambling clinics and hotlines are reporting record levels of appointments and calls.[21]

Gambling addiction among young men is becoming an increasingly alarming issue. I know several friends and acquaintances who place bets daily, often exceeding a hundred dollars each time, without a second thought. Despite lacking the financial means to support these habits, they continue to gamble regularly. For many, placing a bet has become a prerequisite for watching a sports event.

Porn

Since the birth of the internet, people have been complaining about the harm caused by increased exposure to pornography. The unlimited, unrestricted, free access is truly disturbing, especially when we consider the young age at which children are using phones these days. Yes, people might have been able to access porn before, but now they can watch it whenever and wherever they like. Every time they have the urge, they can pick from a million different videos to watch. Additionally, this urge is much likely to be stronger, as people are constantly being pushed sexualized videos on social media because these companies are aware this catches their attention.

The problem with this increased access to porn is that it gives anyone the opportunity to satisfy their sexual needs instantly. People will, and already are, opting to choose the guaranteed result of pornography over the risk of talking to a real-life human being.[22] This dynamic is hurting the success of relationships today and will only continue to harm them as the dating pool becomes people who grew up watching porn instead of learning how to be in a relationship.

Other apps

Whether or not apps are part of the social media landscape, most apps want to keep your attention for as long as possible. For example, *Clash of Clans*, one of the most famous mobile video games of all time, has a feature where you receive additional "gold" through "gold mines" even when you aren't on the app. Every time you open the app, you get to collect the gold, offering a refreshing stimulus mechanism similar to social media. But there comes a point when if you don't log on frequently enough, there is a ceiling to the amount of gold you can collect when away from the app. This forces you to log into the app more frequently to prevent hitting that ceiling and losing out on potential gold. This functionality was designed to keep you addicted to the game. This is a more obvious example of forced addiction, but many other apps have features like daily challenges or frequent notifications, which encourage us to use them. The truth is whatever our vice, whether it's social media, news apps, or video games, the phone is the tool by which we get hooked and stay hooked.

Our phones are obviously having a negative impact on our lives, but it seems like there is no way to limit our addiction. In the next two chapters you will be given the tools to end your phone addiction and improve the quality of your life.

CHAPTER 7

Redesign Your Phone

The reality is that we need our smartphones. Gone are the days when we could get by with a flip phone or even a BlackBerry. Phones are now integral to our society, so I'm not going to encourage you to just get rid of your smartphone. That's not a realistic solution; however, that does not mean we have to continue to use them in the same way.

As we touched on, these massive corporations are not going to change their algorithms anytime soon. There is too much money at stake, so we cannot sit around and wait for a change that will never happen. Nor is legislation likely to come anytime soon. In the last two years, in the US there have been three separate Senate hearings, a surgeon general's advisory on the use of social media, and the surgeon general's call for warning labels on social media apps. That's all well and good, but do you know how much federal legislation has been passed restricting social media and big tech? None, nada, zero. All we have been left with is sound bites on social media that vilify Mark Zuckerberg while, ironically, boosting his net worth.

Like any other addiction, we have to take the issue into our own hands. There is no savior coming to rescue us, and what's really coming is an attempt to addict us further, as corporate profits depend on us maintaining our addiction. Taking this issue into our own hands starts with redesigning our phones to be less addictive devices.

Currently, I would compare our phone to Times Square in New York City. Everywhere we look, we are surrounded by advertisements (app logos and notifications). When our phone is a nonstop marketing extravaganza, it is stimulating and addictive. Instead, we are going to make our phone look peaceful, like Central Park on a Sunday morning. When we make our phones less stimulating and more efficient, we give ourselves a fighting chance to break our addiction.

The following steps are aimed at iPhone users, but those with Android and Samsung devices should be able to replicate these steps easily. Let's walk you through exactly what to do.

STEP 1
Choose dark mode

Admittedly, this is not revolutionary, but it is an important and simple first step in making our phones less addictive. Dark mode is significantly less engaging than light mode on the iPhone. Try it out for yourself as you navigate around your phone using different apps.

Select "Display and Brightness."   Select "Dark Mode."

STEP 2
Delete unnecessary apps

I define unnecessary apps as anything that does not help us communicate with our family and friends, travel, or play music. Everything else can be moved to a separate device. That means ESPN, video games, and the news apps are all unnecessary apps, as they have nothing to do with communication, travel, or music. We may have some other apps like the Find My app (helps find apple devices and air tagged items), but just make sure we don't have too many exceptions.

When we delete certain apps from our phone that doesn't mean we have to stop using them. We can move them to other devices. For example, we can move video games to an Xbox, Netflix to a television, and news to a laptop. You may be thinking, *I have very important things on my phone like my bank account and school emails*. Yes, they are important, but everything doesn't need to exist on our phone. When we keep our entire life on our phone, we are forced to use it. Moving things like our school email to our laptop will be very rewarding, as now school can't follow us everywhere. Additionally, as we move these unnecessary apps to other devices, they won't be immediately accessible or as stimulating, and we will find ourselves using them less and less—or not at all.

STEP 3
Delete all social media apps

Social media qualifies as unnecessary, but its prevalence requires a separate step. It can keep us on our phone for hours, so if we want to decrease our screen time, we must delete these apps. Earlier, I recognized how deleting our social media account is a difficult decision, and some may not be ready for that, so I will recognize this and offer alternatives. However, we need to remove social media apps from our phones. If we still feel the need to access social media, we can do so on our computer. A benefit of this approach is that we will probably find social media less engaging because they are designed for mobile devices and are much clunkier and less enjoyable on laptops.

I deliberately referred to **all** social media here because social media apps are very interconnected. Like any other major industry, when one company succeeds, other companies follow. Earlier, we discussed how Snapchat's success with "stories" led Instagram, Facebook, and YouTube to create their own versions. When similar mechanisms exist across social media, we will find ourselves transitioning our addiction from one app to another. To prove my point, I think many of us have made the transitioned from TikTok to Instagram Reels and found ourselves in the same cycle.

The one account I would definitely recommend deleting is Twitter/X. We have gone over how Twitter/X sucks us into a vortex of biased information, keeps us scrolling for hours, and is not a reliable news source. We can also be comfortable deleting our Twitter/X accounts because it doesn't feel like we are losing our social life.

I suggest we delete our Twitter/X account because it is inaccessible without an account and functions identically on both phone and computer, making it extremely addictive on any device. In comparison, YouTube also runs the same on either platform, but we can still access it regardless of whether we have an account. Therefore, if we delete Twitter/X and have a moment of weakness and search for it, we won't be exposed to its addictive features and unreliable news without an account.

Before you perform the action of deleting these social media apps from your phone, I recommend you read the next step, in which we aim to "destroy" social media from our phones. We will need to keep them downloaded to perform this step.

But before we get there, lets delete the social media aspects of Snapchat while preserving the communication functions.

a. Remove "Stories"

As we discussed earlier, "stories" are extremely harmful. They force us to compare every second of our lives, which ruins our self esteem. If we want to keep Snapchat and be happy, we have to get rid of "stories."

To remove the "story" section is simple: mute every person's "story" or, if they are someone we do not know, remove them as a friend. Some of us may be hesitant to leave "private stories" completely as they are our closest friends, but if our friends really want us to see something, they will send it to us directly.

If you think this step will take too long, I promise it is not as daunting as it seems. It shouldn't take more than five minutes during the first few days to mute the "stories," and from that point on, we will only have to mute a "story" or two now and again. Unfortunately, we cannot do this all at once, as we cannot guarantee that people will post a "story" every day, but the time it takes to do this is worth it.

I cannot emphasize how important this step is, if we plan to keep Snapchat we need to remove "stories." Without removing them, Snapchat is like any other social media app and therefore is extremely harmful to our happiness and productivity.

To mute a "story":

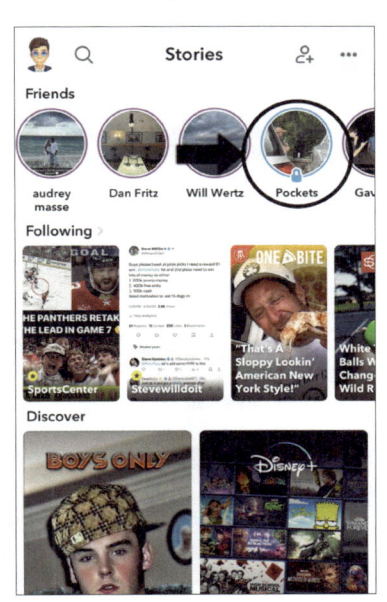

Select a "story" and hold down. 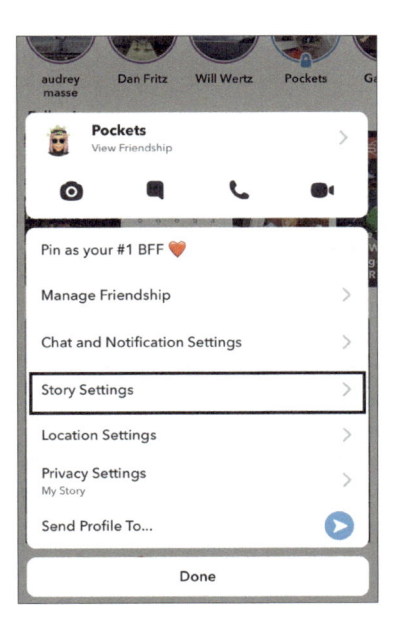   Select "Story Settings."

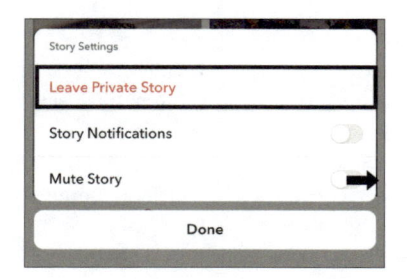

Select "Mute Story" and then "Leave Private Story," if we are on this person's "private story."

We will likely be removing a lot of "stories" at once, so to make this process quicker, select "Mute Story" first then we will be able to stay on this page and click "Leave Private Story" after. If we leave the "private story" first, we will need to go back to the person's page and then select "Mute Story."

To remove a friend:

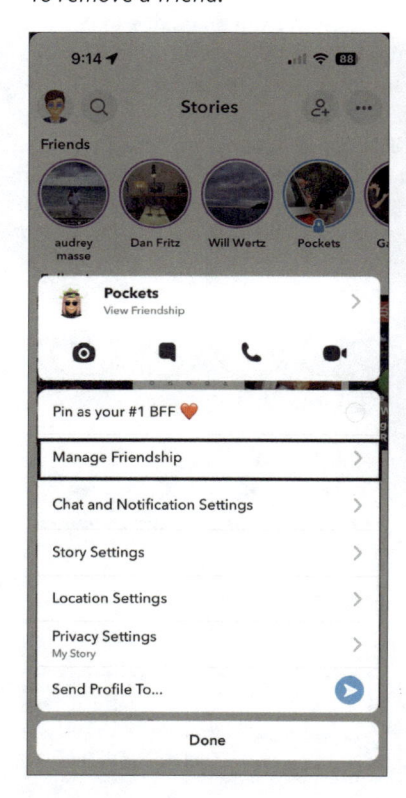

After selecting a "story," select "Manage Friendship" instead of "Story Settings."

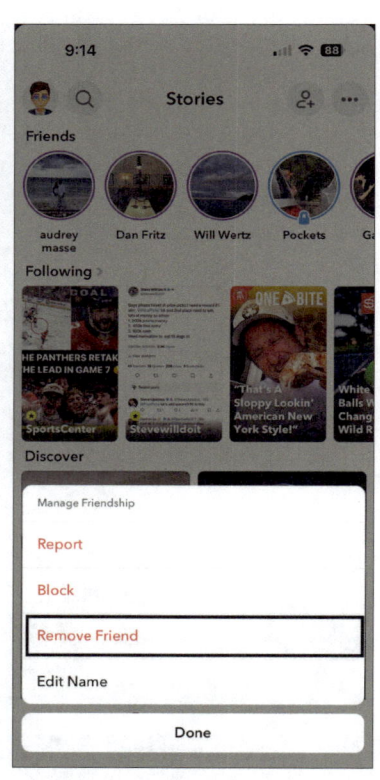

Select "Remove Friend."

b. Remove Following

We can also control the "following" section under "stories." This consists of the people we have added on Snapchat but have not added us. These "stories" have the same effects as others, so we want to get rid of them as well. This also might take a couple of days, as we can't guarantee everyone we are following will post on their "stories" every day.

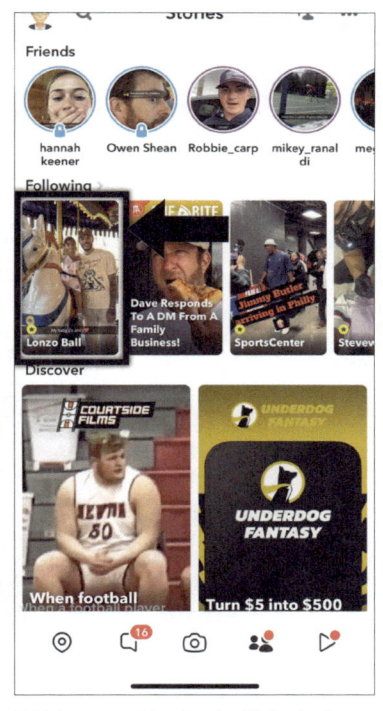

Hold down on a "story" under "Following."

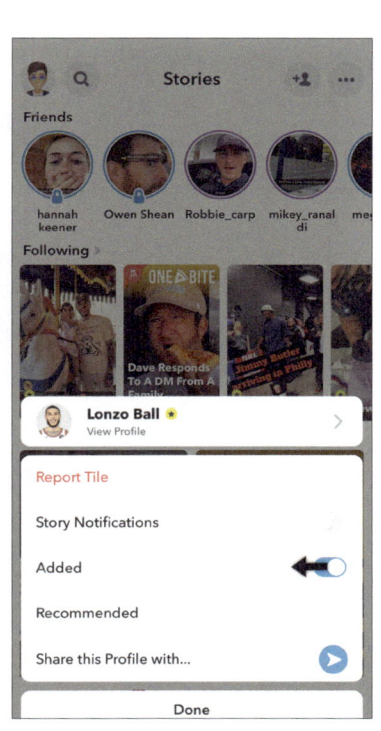

Turn off "Added."

c. Turn off notifications for group chats

I'll talk more about group chat notifications later, but we do not need to be exposed to group chats that most of the time have nothing to do with us. If our friends desperately need us, they will text us individually.

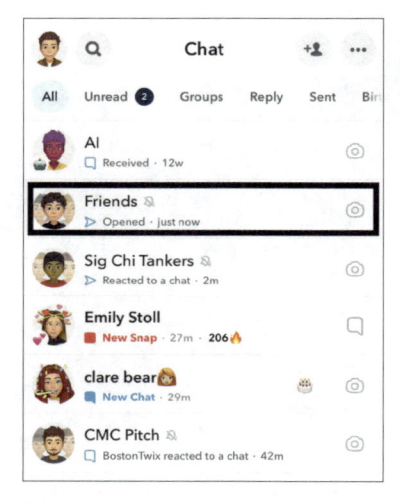

Hold down on a group chat.

Select "Chat and Notification Settings."

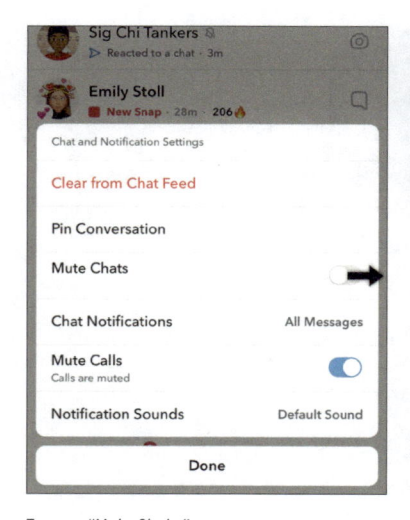

Turn on "Mute Chats."

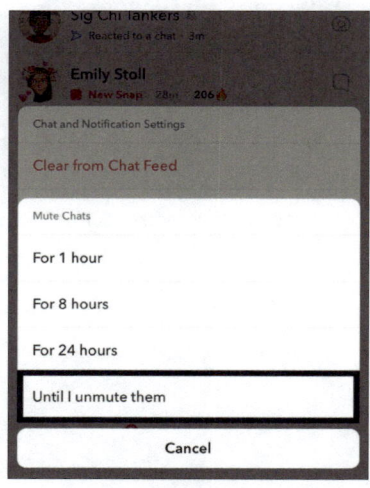

Select "Until I unmute them."

d. Turn off location services

Unfortunately, we cannot disable the maps feature altogether, but we can turn off location services, which prevents us from seeing people's location and the most recent time they have used Snapchat. Turning off location services will also prevent other people from seeing our location.

Open settings and select Snapchat. It will likely be towards the bottom of our settings, so it may be helpful to use the settings search bar.

Select "Location."

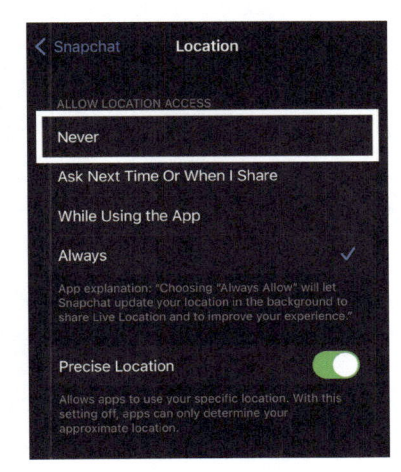

Under location access select "Never."

Redesign Your Phone 61

e. Make Discover Stories less engaging

The only aspect of "stories" that cannot be removed is the "discover stories" section. These exist below our friends' stories and following. We cannot just mute these stories, as Snapchat will continually push us new ones from different accounts. However, we can attempt to minimize their impact.

First and foremost, we want to try to avoid clicking on these stories, but occasionally, we will find ourselves engaged by one of the "discover stories" and click through. After we make this mistake, it is important to ensure this process isn't repeated. We can end the cycle by using the same algorithm meant to distract us to our advantage. Remember, the algorithm thrives on showing us things that keep us engaged, so we are going to trick the algorithm into thinking we dislike things that we actually find engaging.

To do this, every time we find something interesting, we want to click "Hide this Content." This causes the algorithm to think we dislike this type of content, and we will be less likely to see it in the future. If we continue to click "Hide this Content," after a while we will only be recommended "discover stories" that do not interest us.

Find the content we find interesting and hold it down.

Select "Hide this Content."

STEP 4
"Destroy" social media

If you have tried to delete social media apps from your phone, you know it's not that easy. You have probably found yourself redownloading the app or searching the social media on a browser. We are seriously addicted to these apps, so deleting them from our phones is simply not going to be enough. To completely "destroy" social media from our phones, we have to address two things: the ability to redownload the app and the ability to search social media on a browser.

First, I want to recognize the Screen Time Limit feature, as it is the first way most people try to decrease the amount of time they spend on their phones, and it is a feature we will utilize. It seems like an obvious choice to use to decrease phone dependency. Apple graciously built a feature to help us reduce our phone usage; how nice of them! But, wait, Apple doesn't really want us to stay off our phone; they make money off our dependency. This is apparent in the way their screen limit feature was designed.

The Screen Time Limit feature, when used as intended, does a horrible job of preventing us from using apps after we have reached our chosen time limit. When we reach our limit, we can use a passcode to override our limit and access that app again for fifteen minutes, an hour, or the rest of the day. The problem is that it literally takes seconds to unlock the app and start using it again. Let's say we set a time limit on YouTube but we are at the best part of a video and a message appears on our screen blocking our access. Are we going to stop watching the video? Absolutely not! Especially when it only takes us two seconds to enter a passcode to continue watching. Again, we are addicts, a minor inconvenience is not going to stop us. Additionally, when our options are fifteen minutes, an hour, or the rest of the day, we have a lot of time to continue to use these apps. More reasonable times like two or five minutes would be much more efficient at helping us control our usage, but again, Apple doesn't really want that. We can see how this cycle of bypassing the limit repeats until we eventually become sick of the screen time message popping up and just click "approve all day." The idea that Apple created this feature with the intent of actually helping us with our phone usage is a joke.

Even though Apple didn't intend to help us, we can still use this feature to our advantage through one simple trick: have someone else enter the passcode and keep it hidden from us. By allowing someone else to know the passcode, we can no longer instantly override the Screen Limit Feature. Now, when we reach our limit, we will not be able to use the app, which is how it should have been designed in the first place.

With the new trick of having someone else know the password we can use the screen limit feature to minimize our ability to redownload social media. To do this we will set a timer of one minute on all social media apps on our phones. Unfortunately, we cannot set the time limit for zero minutes to completely remove the apps from our phones, but with a one-minute limit we barely have time to use the app after redownloading it and logging in. While not perfect, this hack essentially removes the ability to use these apps on our phone.

After almost completely deleting social media apps from our phones, we have to block the ability to search social media on browsers. After I deleted the Instagram app, searching Instagram on browsers was a much bigger issue for me. Redownloading the app took time and was annoying, but searching the app on Safari or Google took the same minuscule amount of time as entering a passcode. To "delete" the ability to search social media, we simply have to block the websites on our phone. We also need to be unaware of the password for this step because there is an instant override feature for websites as well.

I assume some people, with or without social media addictions, may think these extra steps are ridiculous, but they are necessary. If we don't perform these steps and create barriers for ourselves, I can almost guarantee we will find ourselves using social media on our phone again.

Again, the goal is to delete our social media accounts, as it is the only way to completely end our social media addiction, but if we want to become less addicted without deleting our profile, this is the best way to do it.

To set a Screen Time passcode:

Open settings and select "Screen Time."

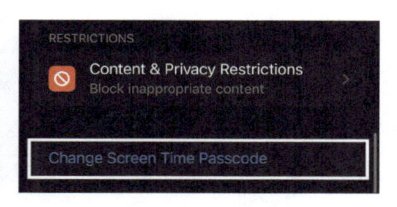

Select "Change Screen Time Passcode" or if you haven't set a password click "Use Screen Time Passcode." Once in this tab we will have to enter our previous password or create a password.

If you don't know your previous password, you will have to reset it with Apple ID. The option to reset with Apple ID only pops up when changing the password, not when you attempting to use the app or website. If it appeared when attempting to use the app or website, overriding with a password would still be easy and make this step pointless.

Once you are ready to enter a password hand the phone to a friend to enter it so you won't know it.

To set limits on apps on your phone:
Remember when I said not to delete social media apps from your phone yet? That is due to this step. To set limits on an app, it has to be downloaded. After, we can delete the app and the limit will still exist if we redownload.

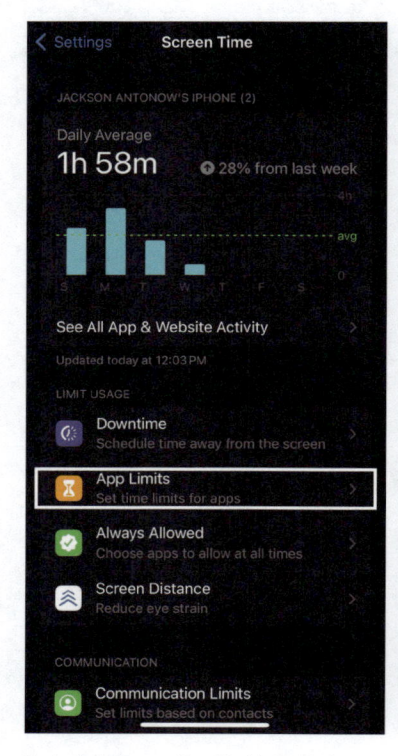

Navigate to "screen time," but instead of selecting "change password", select "App Limits."

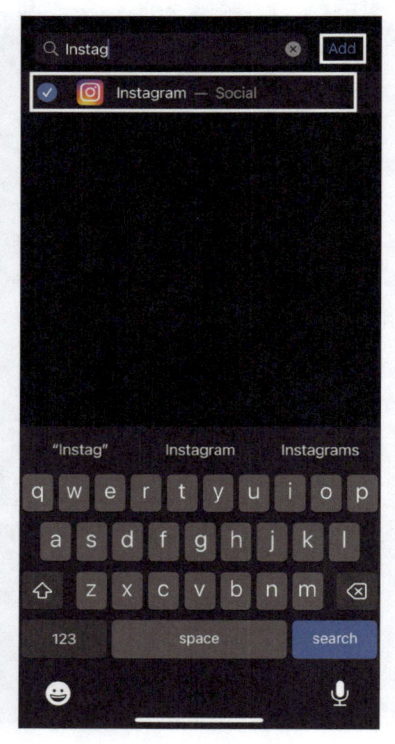

Search the social media apps you want to "destroy" from your phone. We can select under the social category to find these apps, but I find searching for them easier. Once you have found the apps you want to set a limit on, select the tab and then click add in the top right corner.

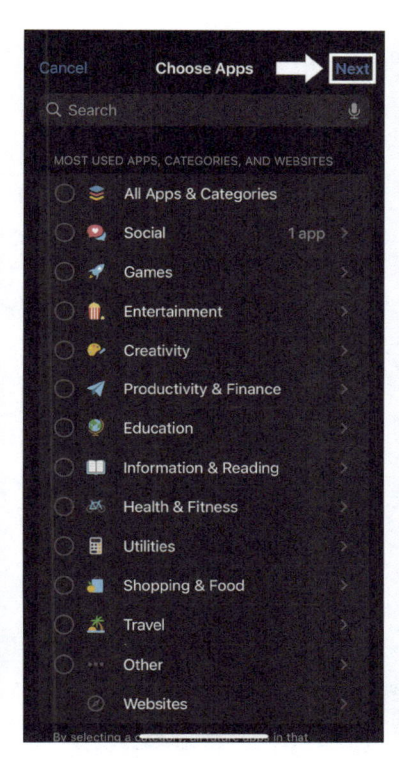

You will be brought back to the "Choose Apps" screen. Select next in the top right corner.

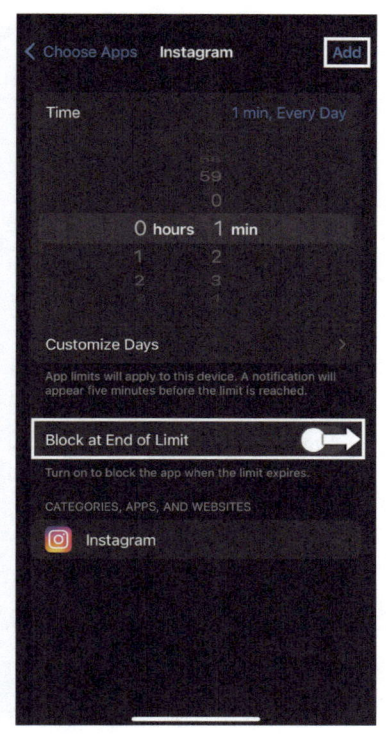

Set the time limit for one minute. If you add a collection of apps you will set the one minute limit for all of them at the same time, but for my example I only did one app. At this screen it is imperative that we **turn on "Block at End of Limit."** If we don't, when our minute is used for the day we will be given an option to bypass the entire limit without a passcode. After selecting "Block at End of Limit," select add in the top right corner.

Now, we can delete the app. Again, if we redownload the app the limit will still exist.

To block social media websites/any website on your phone:

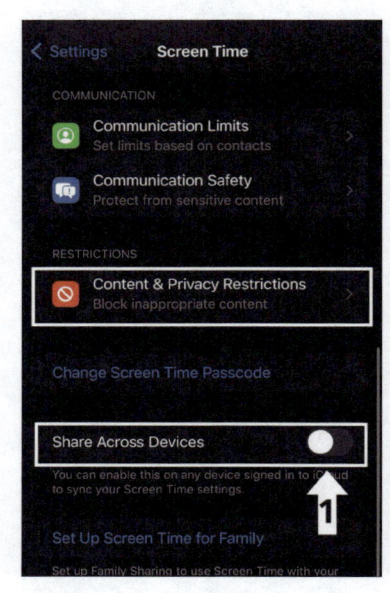

Navigate to "Screen Time" and at the arrow 1, make sure "Share Across Devices" is off. If this is on, then all of the websites that we wish to ban on our phone will also be banned on our other Apple devices with which we use the same Apple account. We may need some customization on a different device, so don't have it automatically carry over.

After this, select "Content and Privacy Restrictions."

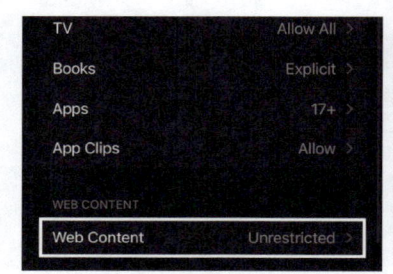

Select "Web Content."

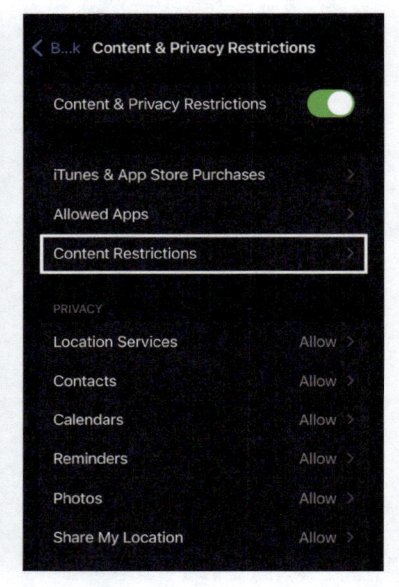

Select "Content Restrictions."

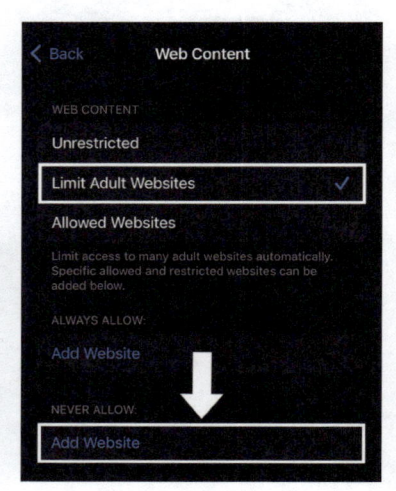

Click "Limit Adult Websites" which allows you to block specific websites. Click "Add Website" under "never allow" and type in the social media websites you want to block.

STEP 5
Remove all remaining apps from the home screen

Remove, but don't delete, all remaining apps from the home screen. This allows us to use our phone without being enticed by app icons. Now we are able to access the Spotify app without scrolling past Snapchat, which would tempt us to use it. You may be wondering, *how do I access apps now?* Simple—just use the search bar. Making this change allows us to use our phone more intentionally and efficiently, exactly how we want to.

If you don't know how to use the search bar, simply slide down when on your home screen.

Arrow 1: To remove an app from our home screen individually, hold down the app we want to remove.

Arrow 2: To remove multiple apps from our home screen at the same time, hold down any area where there's not an app.

Arrow 1: Select "Remove App." After we will be prompted with the screen you see to our right. Select "Remove from Home Screen."

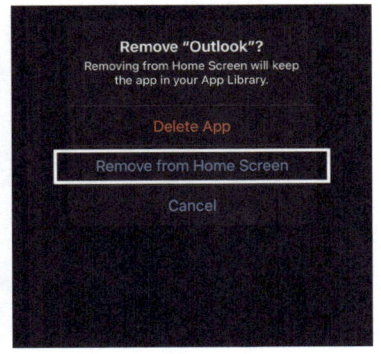

Arrow 2: We will be prompted with the apps shaking with a minus sign on the top right corner, select the minus sign and then we will be prompted with this image. Select "Remove from Home Screen."

Redesign Your Phone

The difference:

Before and after removing apps from our home screen.

STEP 6
Turn off all notifications for non-immediate apps

After we have deleted our social media and other unnecessary apps, we are going to have some apps left over like the App Store, Maps, Spotify, etc. Most of these apps do not require notifications and will fall under the non-immediate app description. A non-immediate app is an app that doesn't require us to give a timely response and therefore does not need to send us notifications. The App Store doesn't need to alert us when a new app is being released, Spotify doesn't need to encourage us to listen to music, and Maps doesn't need to tell us to travel somewhere. These notifications are pure distractions and have no relevance to us.

If we turned off notifications for all apps, we would turn off notifications for apps that we need timely responses for like Snapchat and Messages. If we did this, we would likely find ourselves checking them more often to see if we have received a message. This would defeat the purpose of trying to make us less addicted to our phones. I have attempted to turn off notifications for all apps before, and trust me, it does not work. I found myself checking Snapchat and Messages all the time.

To Turn Off Notifications:

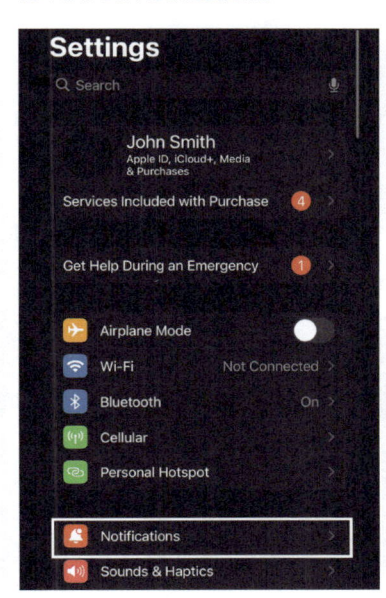

Open settings and select "Notifications."

Select a non-immediate app, like the App Store for example.

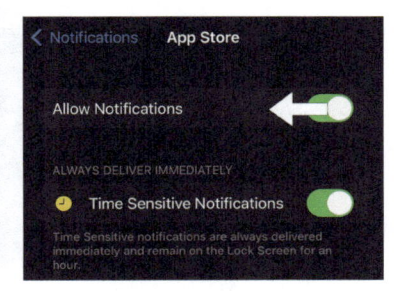

Slide the button off next to "Allow Notifications."

STEP 7
Turn off sound notifications for immediate apps

An immediate app, in contrast, is an app that does require a timely response (for example, Messages, Snapchat, or WhatsApp). For these apps we will keep notifications on but turn off sound notifications.

We do not need to be alerted by a sound every time we receive a notification. Messages or alerts do not require a response the second after they have been sent. We can wait to respond when we reach for our phones later. If we are alerted to our phone by sounds all day, it is impossible to stay focused. We shouldn't be trained to use our phones like we are Pavlov's dog.

If you have a problem with receiving phantom buzzes (the perception your phone is vibrating or ringing when it's not), don't worry you are not going insane. I used to get them all the time. My phone would buzz or ping, yet I would have no notifications. After a week of implementing this step, I no longer had the sensation of receiving these phantom buzzes.

I want to clarify that I do not consider the call feature to be an immediate app. I keep sound notifications on for calls. It is in a category of its own because a call may be important and require an immediate response. A Snapchat or message, on the other hand, can be responded to in a longer time frame, and if we haven't responded quickly enough, then the person will likely call us.

In the ninth step, we turn on "do not disturb," which should mute all sound notifications, but some of our customization of the feature will allow them if we don't turn them off manually. I also wanted to highlight the importance of turning off sound notifications so you can understand why we have made the decision to turn them off.

To turn off sound notifications:

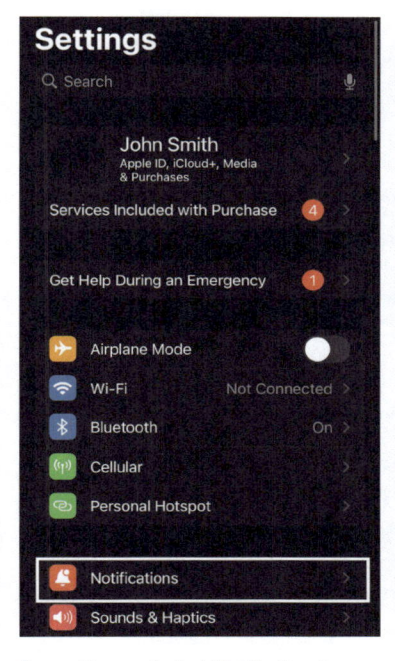

Open settings and select "Notifications."

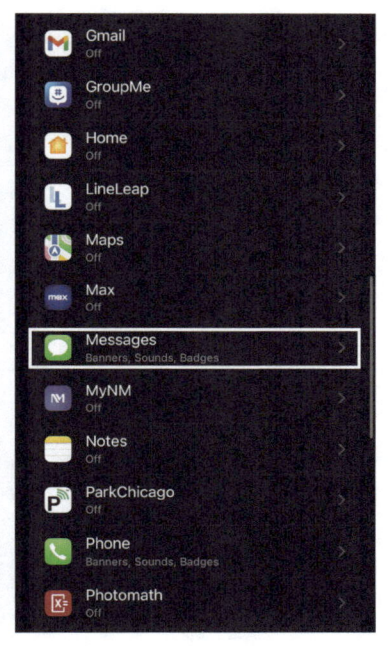

Select an immediate app, like "Messages" for example.

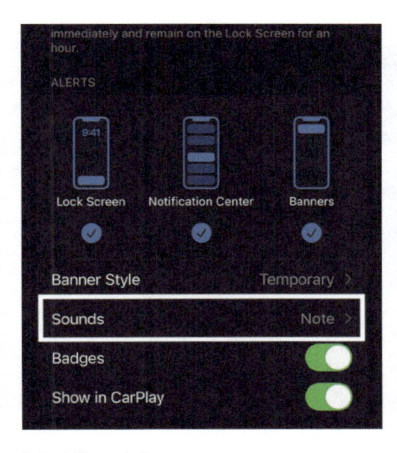

Select "Sounds."

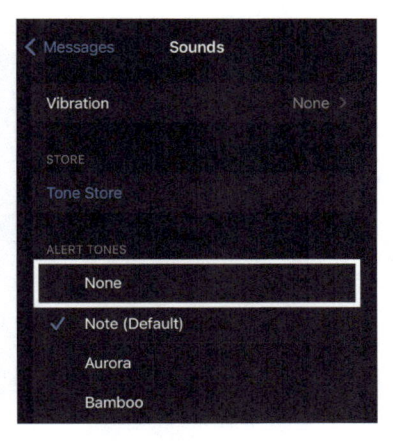

Under Alert Tones, select "None."

Redesign Your Phone   73

STEP 8
Turn off group chat notifications for immediate apps

As we did with Snapchat, we want to turn off group chat notifications because they can go off all day, alerting us to something that does not concern us. For most group chats, what is sent will not require our immediate attention; it will likely be banter or something else that is inconsequential. If someone really needs to speak to us quickly, they will contact us directly. Everything else can be checked on a need-to-know basis.

To turn off group chat notifications:

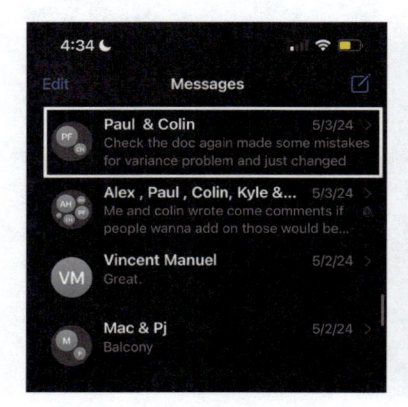

Open messages and select a group chat.

Click the icon at top of the group chat.

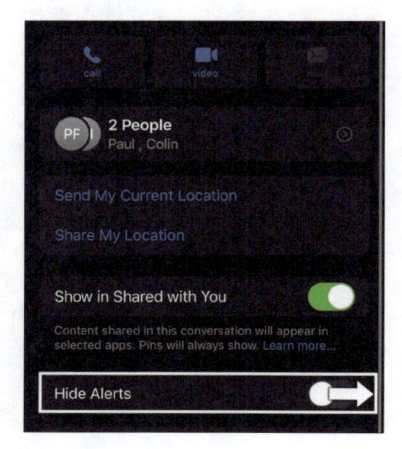

Turn on "Hide Alerts."

74   Enemy in Your Pocket

STEP 9
Use "do not disturb"

Most of us have heard of the "do not disturb" feature and have probably used it before but may not understand why the feature is so beneficial or may have been using it incorrectly. "Do not disturb" gives us control over when we want to see our notifications and allows us to use our phone for a specific purpose. We now can choose the exact app we want without being distracted by notifications, similar to how removing all apps from our home screen stops the temptation of app icons. For example, we can use our phone for directions without seeing Snapchat notifications or use Spotify without being sidetracked by a text message.

We also use "do not disturb" because, again, if we were to just turn off notifications for immediate apps, then we would find ourselves checking these immediate apps more often. "Do not disturb" allows us to keep notifications on for immediate apps without having them control our lives. Like turning off sound notifications, which allowed us to check notifications on our own time, adding the "do not disturb" barrier allows us to check our immediate app notifications when we choose, instead having them pop up on our screen whenever.

To see notifications while in "do not disturb" we simply slide up on the lock screen. While the barrier that "do not disturb" creates for us is great, it can also be abused, which results in many people using the feature incorrectly. A lot of people turn on "do not disturb" but immediately slide up on their lock screen every time they pick up their phone. If we use "do not disturb" in this manner, it becomes a meaningless barrier between seeing notifications immediately and after a millisecond. We want to be conscious of only sliding up on our lock screen when we want to respond, not just when we are seeking a dopamine hit from a notification. "Do not disturb" is only beneficial when we use it precisely.

I do not want us to just turn on "do not disturb"; I want us to set a schedule for keeping this function on indefinitely. We want to always be able to use our phone with purpose and without distraction, not just during certain parts of day. The other benefit to having a schedule is that it prevents us from having to turn on the function manually all the time, which would be annoying, but it is also crucial to limiting our addiction. When we have "do not disturb" scheduled, it allows us to wake up without being bombarded by notifications. Seeing the notifications and then turning on "do not disturb" defeats the purpose of not having the notifications distract us. The morning is when we are likely to have the most notifications because we didn't use our phone for the entire night. It is important to take control of this time.

You may be thinking, *"do not disturb" will never work with my life because I need to know if certain people are trying to get in touch with me.* The great thing about "do not disturb" is that we can choose people to break the feature. When I'm at college, the people who can break my "do not disturb" are my parents and my closest friends. I let my parents break my "do not disturb" because they need to be able to contact me immediately about issues that come up, and I keep my closest friends off "do not disturb" because they need to contact me quite frequently. I don't want to make contacting me feel impossible. If I don't allow my close friends who contact me consistently to evade my "do not disturb," they have to call me twice every time to reach me. Trust me, don't be the guy who is constantly making your friends call you twice all the time; it is annoying.

As our life changes, our break "do not disturb" list should also change. When I go home for the summer, there are different people who need to be in contact with me. I keep my parents on my break "do not disturb," but I add my boss, my coworkers, and home friends who need to be in contact with me, while removing my friends from school. This doesn't mean I stop talking to my college friends, but I am no longer communicating with them about matters urgent to my everday life. They can wait an hour for me to respond. At my summer job, I need my boss and coworkers to become part of my break "do not disturb" because they need to contact me immediately throughout the day. If my boss needed to contact me, but couldn't because I was on "do not disturb," that would probably eliminate my chances of being asked back next summer. Everyone's "do not disturb" list is going to be different, but make sure to select only a certain amount of people. If we include everyone, then we have defeated the purpose of trying to control our notifications.

It is important to note that the people who can break our "do not disturb" can only do so through messages and calling. So, if somebody sends us a Snapchat who we have on break "do not disturb," that notification will not bypass "do not disturb." I personally like this feature because messages and calls normally contain more important information than my Snapchat messages.

The last thing I will mention about "do not disturb" is that we can adapt it for different devices. I have two Apple products: my phone, which I use to communicate, and my computer, which I use for school and work. Each device has a different break "do not disturb" list. On my phone, as we just discussed, I have a specific break "do not disturb" list, but on my computer, no one is on that list. This is intentional because when I am on my computer I am doing school work and do not need any outside distractions.

Set Up Do Not Disturb Schedule Steps:

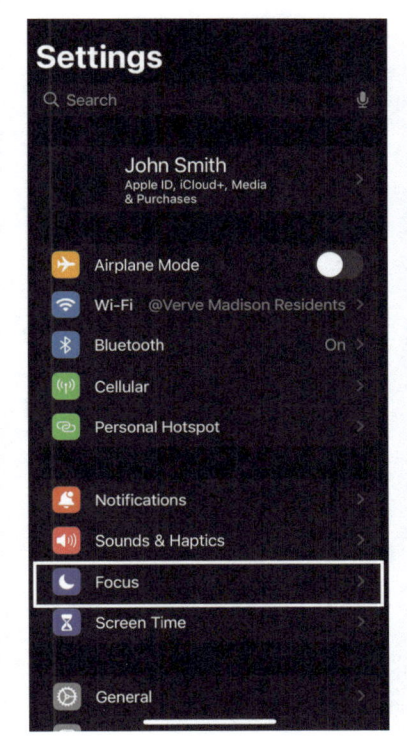

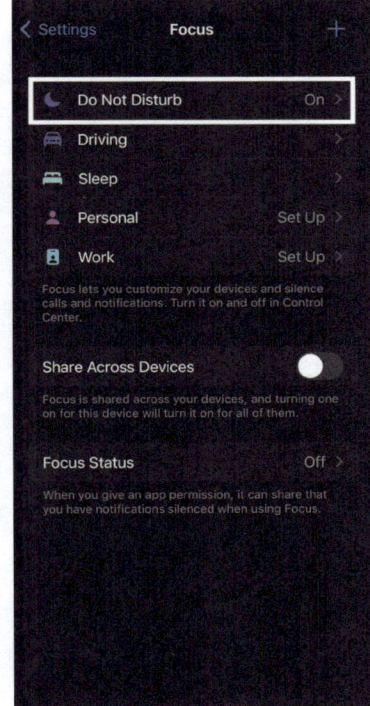

Open settings and select "Focus."

Click "Do Not Disturb."

Redesign Your Phone 77

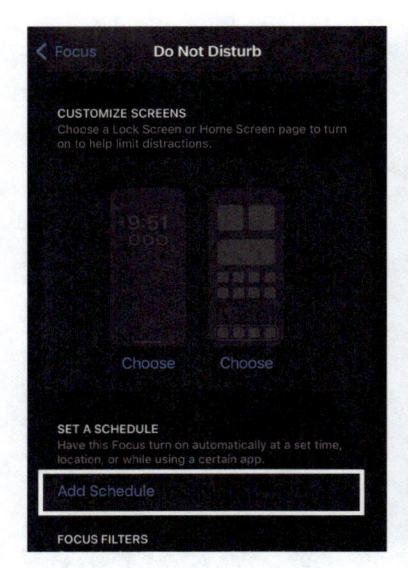

Scroll down and select "Add Schedule."

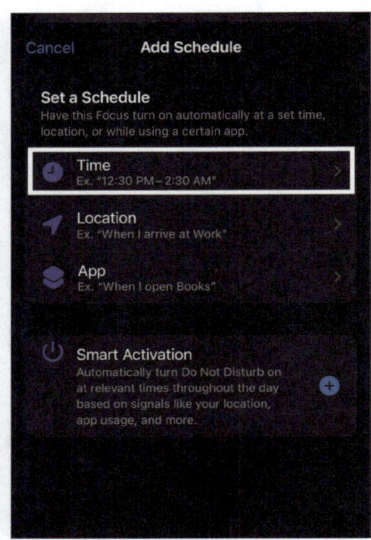

Select "Time."

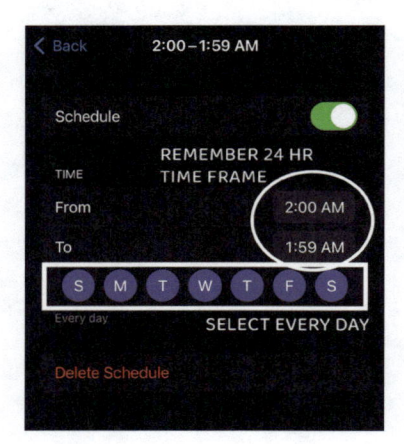

Choose a 24-hour time frame, technically a 23 hour and 59 minutes time frame, that resets at a time when we plan to be asleep. This allows "do not disturb" to be running all the time when we are awake. Also make sure to select every day of the week.

Set Up People to Break Do Not Disturb Steps:

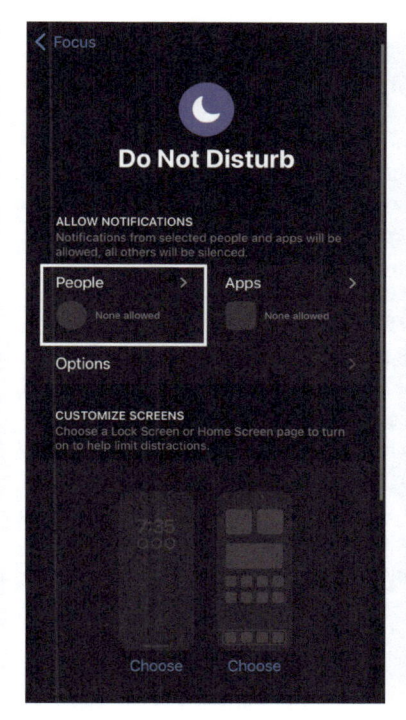

Navigate back to the "do not disturb" home page. Select the "People" tab.

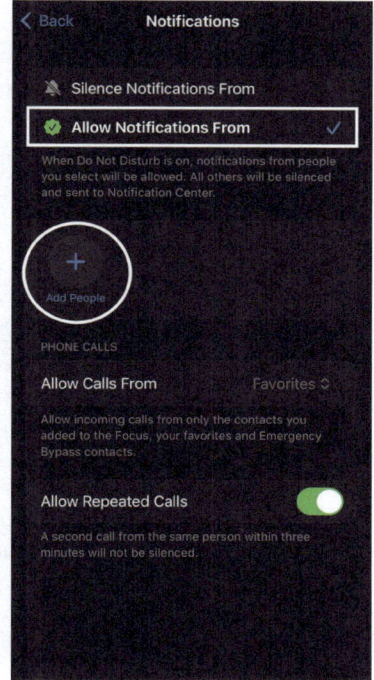

To allow people to break our "do not disturb" first select "Allow Notifications From." Then select "Add People" and choose the people we want to break our "do not disturb."

STEP 10
Use a screen time widget

A screen time widget allows us to track the time we spend on our phone throughout our day and week. It is perfect because it only tracks the time we actively spend on our phone. So, if we are responding to messages that will count towards our screen time, but if we are just using our phone to listen to music then it won't count towards it.

Having this feature allowed me to be accountable and only use my phone for an hour each day. If I feel I have already used my phone for a long time, I always swipe left to my screen time widget. If I see I have used my phone for thirty minutes by 12:00 p.m., I know it is time for me to do something else. I also like the screen time widget because it helped track my progress. It reminded me that I was making progress towards my goal of lower screen time, and helped me to not get discouraged. Seeing myself drop from a screen time of eight hours to only an hour was extremely motivating when I was trying to end my addiction.

It is important to be careful while using this feature, as it can be misused. If we set a goal of less than an hour a day, that doesn't mean we have to use it for at least an hour. We shouldn't scramble to use up our "allowed minutes." For example, if we have used our phone for only ten minutes at 9:00 p.m. that doesn't mean we should use our phone for fifty minutes straight before we fall asleep.

Bear in mind, too, that our screen time might not give a true reflection of how we are using our phone. For example, we may use our phone to watch a movie on an airplane or to Facetime someone. That time we spent watching a movie or Facetiming a friend will increase our average time for the day but is not a true reflection of how we are improving our phone addiction. In these situations, we should pay attention to the time we spend on our phone without counting the Facetime call or movie. Avoiding calling our friends or sitting in silence on an airplane just to meet a screen time goal hurts our quality of life, which is what we're trying to improve. If we do this, we let an arbitrary number control us instead of focusing on improving our happiness. Screen time is a guide, not the definitive representation of our phone usage.

Screen time widget steps:

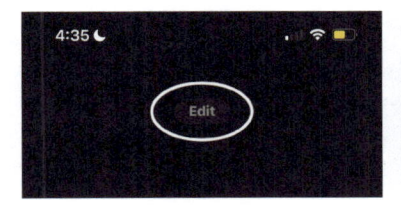

Swipe all the way left on the home screen and select "Edit."

Select the plus sign in the top left.

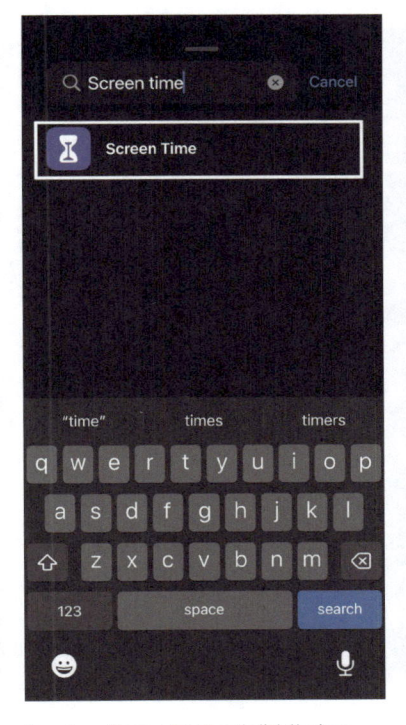

Search up "Screen Time" and click the icon.

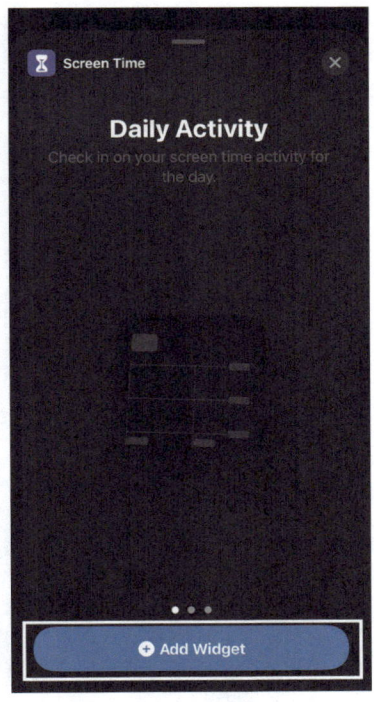

Select "Add Widget."

Redesign Your Phone   **81**

STEP 11

Use a night shift schedule

Apple's night shift schedule allows us to "warm" our phone brightness before bed, which is supposed to help us have a better sleep. I like this feature because seeing that my phone has turned "warmer" signals to me that it is time to stop using my phone. It also makes our phones a little less addicting before bed.

Night Shift Schedule Steps:

Open up settings and select "Display and Brightness."

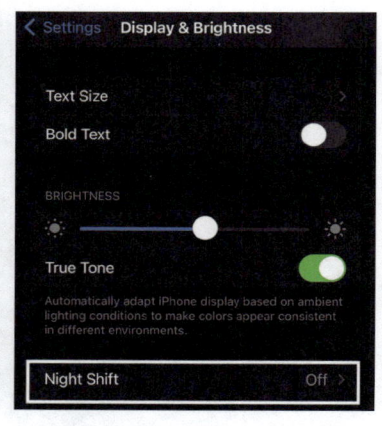

Scroll down and select "Night Shift."

After turning on "Scheduled," select "From To". We will automatically be prompted with the 9pm to 7am tab, but if we select this tab it will allow us to set our own time.

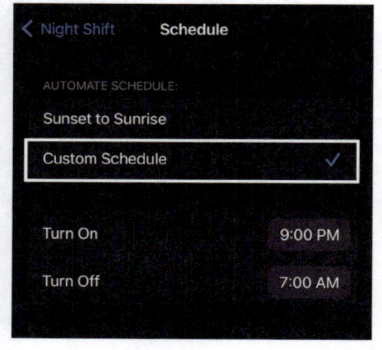

Set a time that is around an hour before you put your phone away for the night and turns off before you wake up. Also make sure the color temperature is set to as warm as possible.

Enemy in Your Pocket

STEP 12
Use grayscale (optional)

Grayscale will display our iPhone in black and white, which makes it extremely boring. If we perform all of the previous steps and use grayscale, we may find ourselves using our phones less than ten minutes a day. Personally, though, I don't enjoy grayscale. When I FaceTime my friends, or my mother sends me photos, I like to see those images in color. Still, I wanted to make this feature known to you, as you may end up using it.

Grayscale steps:

Open settings, scroll down and select "Accessibility."

Select "Display and Text Size."

Select "Color Filters."

Turn on color filters and then select "Grayscale."

Redesign Your Phone   83

STEP 13
Change settings on other connected devices

While I have argued the phone is the main problem in the world of technology, I would be remiss to not mention other potentially harmful devices. The heart of Apple is the interconnectedness of its software. When we receive a message on one Apple device, we receive it on all Apple devices. A message or FaceTime that we received on our phone will also be received on our computer. When I moved away from aimlessly responding to messages on my phone, I started to do it on my computer when I was trying to get work done. That is why I recommend we remove FaceTime and Messages from our computer.

Some people may be hesitant to remove Messages or FaceTime on their computer, but trust me, this is a change for the better. When we are on our computer, it should be time for us to be focused on work or school, not respond to messages or FaceTimes. We can respond to these notifications later on our phone. (See Figure 1 to remove Messages and Figure 2 to remove FaceTime.)

Besides Messages and Facetime, I also found myself checking LinkedIn (a social media I haven't deleted) on my computer when I didn't want to. When we don't delete social media accounts, they can suck us in on other devices. If we don't want to delete a social media account but still find ourselves using them on our computer, then blocking the websites on specific browsers could help.

I say specific browsers because for an app like LinkedIn, we still may need to log in every now and again. If we block LinkedIn on the browser we choose to do our schoolwork on, then it may dissuade us from using it when are trying to accomplish something. When we need to use LinkedIn, we can search it on another browser. At a certain point, though, we do have to try to summon some willpower if we decide to not delete our social media accounts. (See Figure 3 to block websites.)

Finally, using YouTube mindlessly on my computer was also an issue. The problem is, as we identified earlier, unlike other social media where if we delete our account we are unable to use the platform, YouTube will always grant us access. The good news is there is a way to remove YouTube's recommended videos, the refreshing function that makes it so addicting. Making this change allows us to use YouTube intentionally instead of getting sucked down a never-ending rabbit hole. (See Figure 4 to remove YouTube Video Recommendations.)

Figure 1: To remove messages on computer:

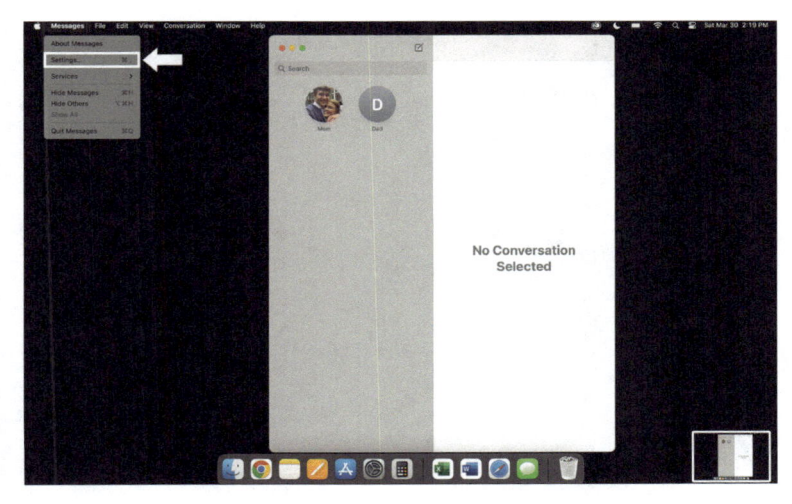

Open Messages, select "Messages" in the top left corner, and then select "Settings."

We will then be prompted with this screen, select "iMessage", and then next to the Apple ID select "Sign Out."

Figure 2: To remove Facetime on computer:

Open Facetime, then click "Facetime" in the top left corner, and then click "Turn Facetime Off."

Figure 3: To block websites:

To block websites on Safari:
Open up "Settings" on your Apple computer and follow the same steps we did for the phone when blocking websites. Unfortunately, unlike the iPhone where blocking a website blocks it for all search engines, when we perform this step on the Apple computer it will only block websites on Safari.

To block websites on Google Chrome:

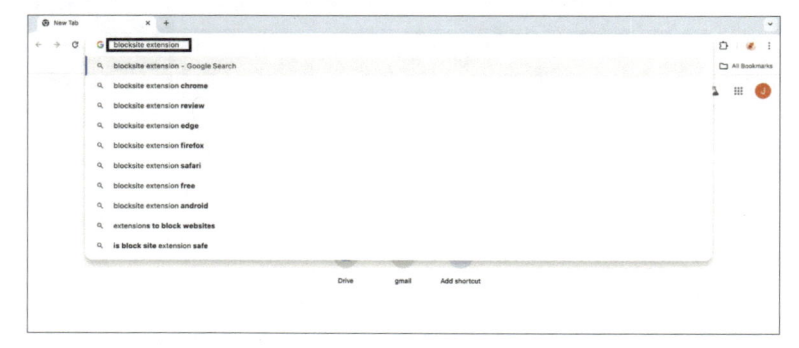

Search up "BlockSite extension" on Google Chrome.

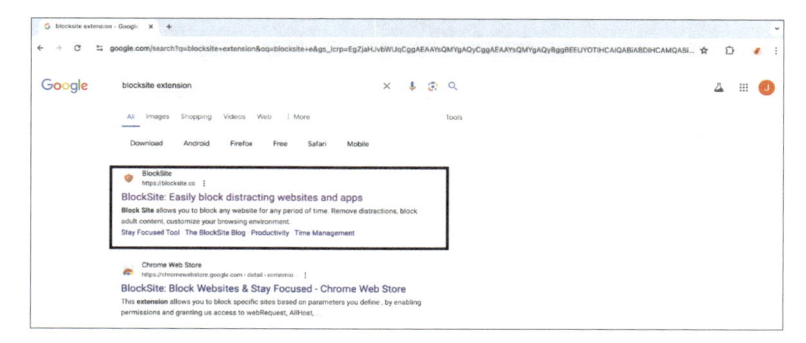

Select the BlockSite link.

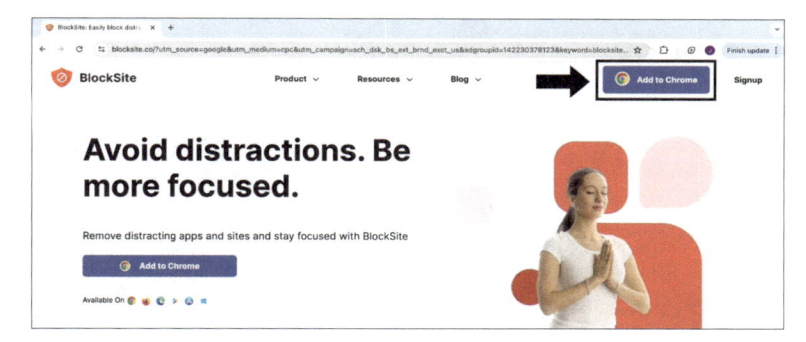

Select "Add to Chrome". After this step we will be brought to the Google Chrome store, just hit 'Add to Chrome" again.

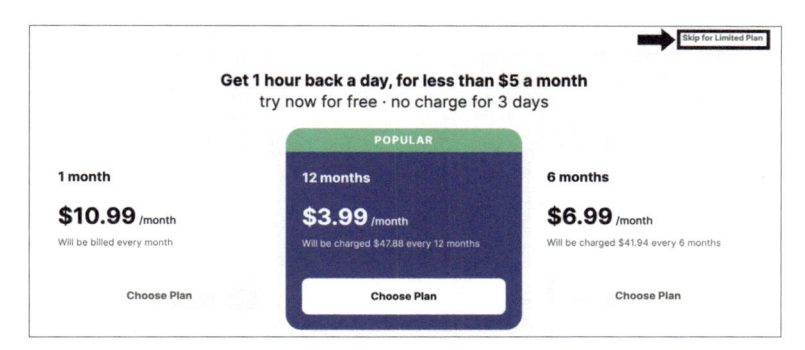

After downloading the extension, we will go through the process of setting up BlockSite on our computer. It may seem like we have to pay for this service, but we do not. Select "Skip for Limited Plan" in the top right corner which allows us to block up to three websites, which should be plenty.

Redesign Your Phone 87

Figure 4: To remove YouTube video recommendations:

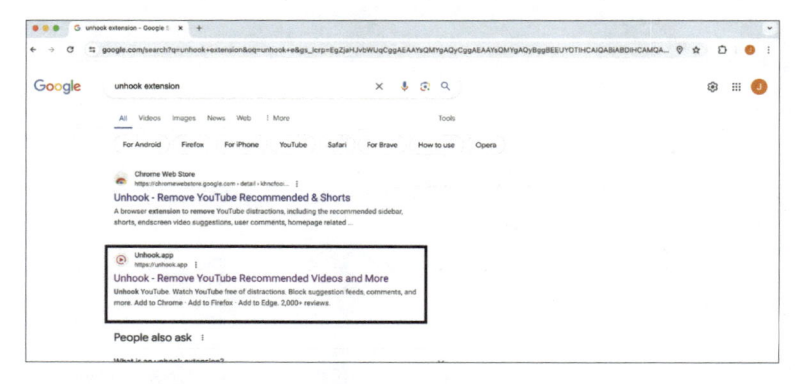

Search "Unhook extension" on Google Chrome, Firefox, or Microsoft Edge.

Once on the Unhook website, we can remove YouTube recommendations on our selected website by clicking any of the three browser icons. I use Google Chrome, so I selected that icon.

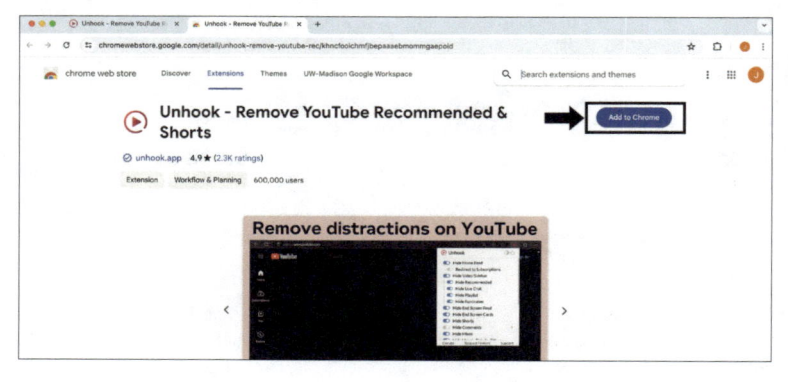

Selecting the Google Chrome icon will lead us to the Google Play Store where we can click "Add to Chrome". We now will no longer be recommended YouTube videos without searching them directly.

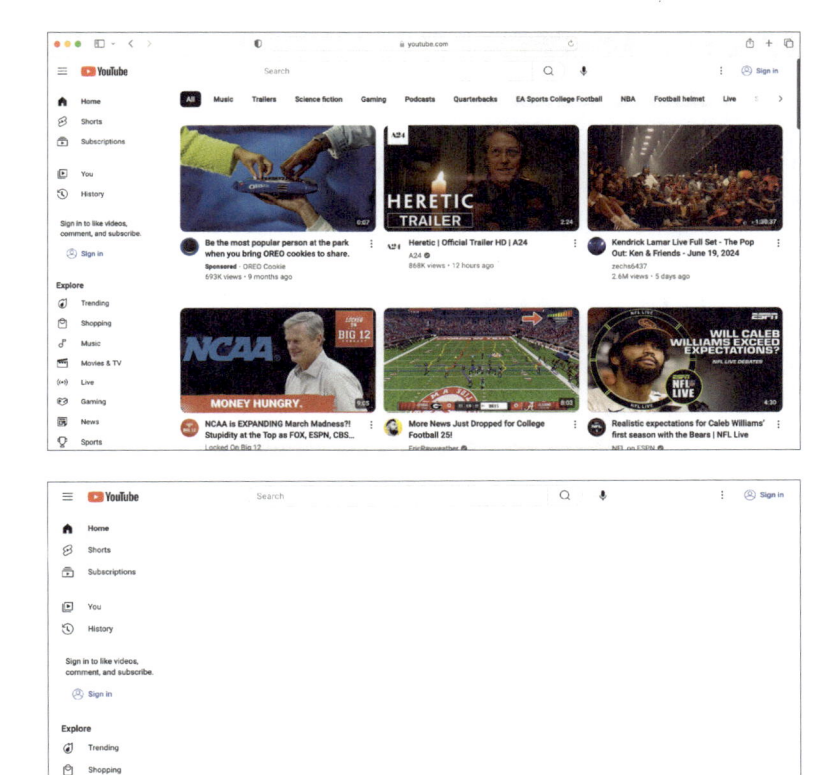

Before and after removing video recommendations.

Redesign Your Phone   89

CHAPTER 8

Changing Our Habits

Changing the way our phone is designed will not guarantee an end to our addiction. In the same way that drug addicts with money problems still find a way to get their next hit, we can still find a way to be addicted to our phone even after we have made it extremely difficult. We have to make an effort to change our habits if we want to end our phone addiction once and for all.

STEP 1
Use our phone with intention

Next time we pick up our phone, we should know our purpose in using it. By doing this, we decrease our chances of getting inadvertently distracted. If we find ourselves picking up our phones without a purpose, then we know we are just chasing a dopamine high.

For example, one purpose of using our phone could be to get directions. We have to be clear about our intentions because phones, again, are different from other technologies; they have endless possibilities. If we don't establish our intentions, we may find ourselves responding to Snapchats instead of using our phone for directions. You may notice that without redesigning our phone, it is almost impossible to use our phone with intention. We will be alerted with notifications or see the logos of other apps, constantly enticing us away from our original goal. Redesigning our phone and changing our habits go hand in hand.

STEP 2
Only send necessary texts

Once we have redesigned our phone, texts should be the only thing with potential for recurring stimulus. Social media and video games won't be able to give us new posts or objectives, but texts can always refresh as people need to contact us. Earlier, we talked about how when we delete a social media app we could find ourselves looking for another social media to satisfy our addiction (the transition from TikTok to Instagram Reels). If we aren't careful, we might find ourselves manically texting as a way to replace our social media addiction.

To control this, we simply need to send fewer texts (messages, Snapchats, etc.). It sounds obvious, but the fewer texts we send, the fewer we will receive. If we sent a text to a friend, they are more likely to text us than if we hadn't texted them at all. This was one of the most helpful tips I took away from the book *Indistractable* by Nir Eyal.[23] *Indistractable* also focuses on technology addiction and was one of the inspirations for me to write this book.

You may be thinking, *all the texts I send my friends are necessary*, but they aren't. We don't need to text our friends about everything that happens to us. Who we saw at lunch or a funny video we saw on Instagram are not things we need to send to people. These moments will be forgotten in an hour.

We need to redefine how we are communicating with our friends. Previously, I mentioned how we judge our romantic relationships based on how often we text each other, and some of us have the same problem with friendships. Again, constant messaging is not a barometer of the success of a relationship. We all have friends who we haven't talked to for years but instantly get along with when we see them again.

So, what counts as a necessary message? It is any message that helps us meet up with our friends in person. Currently, we use our phones as a tool to hang out with friends virtually, when it should be the tool to meet up with friends in person. If we want to talk with a friend but can't meet up in person, I encourage us to call them. A call serves as a one-off conversation, while conversations through text can last the whole day and repeatedly distract us. The other benefits of phone calls are that they are more personal and we will likely find ourselves more engaged in the conversation.

Now sometimes we will send texts that are not worth a phone call like, "Have you done the math homework?" or "Can you get me this from the store?" but try to keep these types of texts to a minimum. Again, the more we send, the more we will receive.

STEP 3
Use the "ride the wave" technique

I am also stealing this idea from *Indistractable*. When I started the process of curing my phone addiction, this technique was instrumental. It works like this: every time we feel the urge to go on our phone, we tell ourselves to wait five more minutes. By then, the urge will likely have gone away. If the feeling hasn't passed in five minutes, we tell ourselves the same thing and wait five more minutes. This technique seems a little bit funky at first, but I promise it works. About 99.9 percent of the time, my urge is completely gone after the first five minutes.

Every time we use this technique, it's a small victory in our battle against our addiction. We can feel our mind becoming stronger and less addicted to our phone every time we resist. I loved knowing that every time I resisted, I was improving my life. At first we will probably use "ride the wave" all the time, but the more we use it, the less addicted we will become. Eventually, it won't be a conscious thought to not use our phone.

STEP 4
Completely power down our phone when we are not using it

Powering off our phone makes our phone take more time to use, which makes it more bothersome to access and less addictive. It creates a barrier for us that doesn't allow us to use our phone immediately. It is easier to stay off our phone when we can't instantly pick it up and start using it.

Although powering it on might take only ten seconds, the time it takes forces us to think more about what we are doing. I use this trick every day, whether it is when I want to focus or when I am in a conversation with friends. When trying to focus, there have been many times when I reached for my phone, realized it was powered off, and decided not to go through the trouble of turning it on. Just as often, while attempting to focus, I have reached for my phone, realized it was turned on, and then became distracted. In social situations, I power off my phone because it forces me to be present with my friends. When my phone is powered off, it's harder for me to use it, which compels me to stay engaged in conversations or find new ones, instead of scrolling awkwardly in the corner. This trick is awesome and one of the easiest to start practicing.

STEP 5
Don't use our phone during every reset period

A reset period is the moment between finishing one thing and starting another. For example, it is the moment between finishing our homework and watching TV or the moment between the end of a sports practice and driving home. For me, and a lot of other people, this is when we reach for our phones. In high school, the second I was done with anything—basketball practice, homework, a movie—I would check my phone. Again, the goal is to use our phones when we need to, not because we are searching for a dopaime high.

The idea is simple: we make a conscious effort to not use our phone after finishing a task. This is easy in theory, difficult in practice. To help yourself, think, *I will use my phone in a future reset period*. For example: instead of checking your phone after sports practice, check it when you get home. Or check your phone once you get to work instead of the second you get up. Keep on attempting to push your phone usage to a future period. The benefit of this strategy is that we will find ourselves able to accomplish more tasks continuously. Instead of waking up, phone, eating, phone, school, phone, working out, phone, we can now do multiple things in a row.

Another way to help ourselves is to not respond to everything on our phone before we start doing something. When we respond to everything, it primes our phone to be as engaging as possible when we pick it back up. For example, if I respond to my ten best friends on Snapchat before setting down my phone, I am likely to receive a notification from at least some of them when I use it again. If we send only necessary messages (Step 2), we will likely have fewer notifications and our phone will be less engaging next time we pick it up.

STEP 6
Understand that we do not need to reply immediately

Whether it's social media, messages, or phone calls, there is an expectation that we must respond immediately. It is important to realize that what happens on our phone does not need to be responded to in that exact second. Remember why we turned on "do not disturb": to regain control over when we want to respond to our notifications, rather than having to see them instantly.

To help us delay our response time, it's worth thinking through what we gain from responding to a notification. It's a huge dopamine hit, yes, but how does it help us besides causing a temporary, manufactured improvement in mood? We will receive thousands of notifications in our life, responding to one notification at 12:00 p.m. on a Tuesday is not something to worry about.

You may currently be in a relationship built around a constant communication style and feel that not responding instantly is unrealistic. If you are in this situation, it's a good idea to have an open and honest conversation with your significant other. We have talked about how this communication style is unhealthy, and straying from it can lead to a better relationship. Communicating less frequently removes the stress of feeling that we have to respond, and when we aren't constantly texting our significant other, we will have more to talk about when we see them in person. Don't ignore this step just because your girlfriend/boyfriend expects you to respond instantly.

Other things also don't need to be responded to immediately. News alerts can wait, as they will still be there when you check them later. If you have decided to keep video games on your phone, specific objectives can be addressed another time. Finally, we don't need to ask Google a question the second it pops into our head. I am an inquisitive person, and when I used my phone frequently, every time I wondered about something, I would use my phone to answer the question. "How many points is LeBron James averaging?" "What school did person X go to?" "Who was the first person to step foot on the moon?" Most of the questions we have, our phones can answer, but we don't need to know information immediately or sometimes at all.

STEP 7

Understand that checking our phone cannot fix our current situation

At the height of my phone addiction, I found myself reaching for my phone whenever I felt anxious or stressed. When I was in an uncomfortable social situation, I would check my phone in an attempt to remove my feelings of awkwardness. When I was doing schoolwork and unable to comprehend a topic, I would check my phone so I could avoid trying to understand it. When I was unhappy, I would stress-scroll through Instagram so I didn't have to think about it. In all of these situations, my phone provided some temporary relief, but it didn't change my current situation. I still felt awkward, was still unable to understand the topic, and was still unhappy. When we understand that our phone can't fix our problems, we will be less inclined to reach for it as a security blanket.

STEP 8

Do not leave our phone in our bedroom at night

I came to realize I was addicted to my phone when I found that I couldn't fall asleep without it and would reach for it as soon as I woke up. My day started and ended with my phone; it was as if my very existence was connected to it.

Keeping our phone away from our bedroom is the best way to stop this habit. It reinforces that our nights and mornings are for us and not the outside world. For those who say, "I need my phone as an alarm," go buy a $10 alarm. For those who say, "I need my phone for white noise," go buy a white noise machine. We can think of a million excuses to keep our phone in our room, but we just don't need it there.

STEP 9

Don't use our phone first thing in the morning

This is made much easier by keeping our phone out of our bedroom, but it is still possible to start using it first thing in the morning. Unless we make a conscious effort, we can find ourselves waking up and sprinting toward our phone.

To help achieve this, roughly plan what you want to do before using your phone. I say "roughly" because I was always annoyed by people who recommended extremely strict regimens to break my phone addiction. Putting my life on a uncompromising plan to break my phone addiction was not attractive, as the goal of breaking my phone addiction was to improve my life, not make it worse. An example of a "rough" schedule involves thinking, *I'm going to go through my morning routine, eat breakfast, do some work, and then check my phone.*

A lot of coffee drinkers become addicted to caffeine because they get into the habit of drinking it in the morning. We do the same thing when we use our phones first thing, and it sets a precedent for us to use our phones for the rest of our day. If we can cut out phone usage in the morning, we will be less likely to use the device as often later in the day.

Another thing that happens when we use our phone first thing is we commit ourselves to laziness. We take away our ability to start our days, as our phones keep us in our beds instead of putting us on our feet. It is impossible to start our day off on a productive note when we spend the first thirty minutes of it scrolling.

STEP 10
Do not take our phone everywhere

Right now, we probably believe it's necessary to take our phone everywhere, but we don't have to. There are a ton of places where our phone isn't needed. We don't need to bring our phones to go to 7-Eleven, the library, to take a shower, to shop at the grocery store, and in so many other situations. We may bring our phone to a lot of places for music, but remember, not every single moment requires us to have music playing.

You may be thinking, *I need to bring my phone; someone might need to reach me*. Do you really believe that? Are you really so important that you have to be available 24/7? Unless you are the President of the United States, you cannot convince me that you *need* to be contacted. We can wait thirty minutes to respond to our friends.

Another concern that people have is safety. If they don't bring their phone everywhere, they won't have the ability to call someone if they are in danger. I promise you, you won't be attacked every time you leave your house. Do we live the rest of our lives in constant fear? We don't stop eating because we may choke, stop swimming because we may drown, or stop playing sports because we may tear our ACL.

The final concern is that there might be an emergency. I am constantly told, "I need my phone. What if my family is in an emergency?" I want us to think of how many times we have been called about an actual emergency—not a friend asking for help with a breakup or our parents asking about filling out a form for school, but a real emergency, one where someone was in real trouble. For most of us, the number of emergencies has probably been either zero or one. The concern of an emergency connects to both our worries about our perceived safety and anxieties of believing someone will need to contact us. No one needs to contact us immediately and the people around us are most likely safe. Living our lives with the expectation that we need to be contacted, are in danger, or our family is at risk of injury or abuse is not only unrealistic but also makes us terrified of the world. Why would we do anything or go anywhere if someone needs us, we might be attacked, or our family might have been taken hostage? These outlier events of tragedy happen maybe once in a lifetime, but we act as if they are about to happen every other second. There is no reason for our phones to always be on us despite what our anxieties might tell us.

STEP 11
When we bring our phone somewhere, make it less accessible

At the same time, there are some places we need to bring our phones. We may need them for directions or to communicate with people when we are on the go. But when we do bring them, let's make our phones less accessible. Put it somewhere where it is hard to reach and, therefore, hard to start using again. By making our phones less accessible, we create a barrier to using them, similar to what we do when we power off our phones.

There are a few ways to start practicing this. We can bring our phone on a walk but leave it in our backpack, bring our phone to an appointment but leave it in the car, or bring our phone to the gym for music, but leave it in a cubby if we have Bluetooth headphones.

Even when we are in our homes, we can practice this. When we are watching a movie, we can put our phone in a different room. When we have friends over, we can all put our phones in a cabinet. We don't need our phones to text anyone because we are already with the people we want to be with. Our focus should be on them, not our mobile device.

STEP 12
Replace screen time with other activities

This is a more obvious recommendation, but we need to find new hobbies to fill the newfound time in our life. If we don't, we will likely find ourselves gravitating towards our phone again when we have nothing to do. Breaking our addiction is going to be hard when a phone is our only outlet for curing boredom.

Start working out, reading, watching TV or movies, playing billiards—anything that you think you might enjoy. It doesn't have to be groundbreaking, just simple activities that keep you away from your phone. Throughout my life, I have always wanted to read books but never felt like I had the time or the ability to focus for long periods of time. From ages fourteen to nineteen, I read around three books—yes, including in school. Now, in the past year, I've read over twenty books, something that my younger self would not have believed.

I mentioned TV or movies as a hobby, which may come as a surprise to some. While TV can be a huge time waster, it at least beats being on your phone. Again, this book is not meant to make your life miserable. Your new hobbies don't have to be waking up at 5:00 a.m., running marathons, reading a book every week, and meditating. We don't need to live an intense lifestyle to break our phone addiction.

The days when I use my phone the least are when I am keeping myself busy. When I have things to do, my screen time is under an hour without even thinking about it. When I sit at home after work or school, I find my screen time is closer to the two-hour mark, and thinking about my phone more often. Find new hobbies that you enjoy, and do them!

STEP 13
Do not use a phone wallet

This may seem like a minor change, but it is actually very important. One of our goals is to make our phones less integral to our everyday lives. However, when we have IDs and credit cards attached to or on our phone, it becomes essential. We can't go anywhere without our phones when our wallet is attached to them because then we can't identify ourselves or pay for anything. We should ditch the wallet on the back of our phone, or remove our mobile credit cards and start carrying a physical wallet.

STEP 14
Understand this is not a quick and easy process

Overcoming any addiction is difficult, and phone addiction is no different. Again, the most valuable companies in the world are doing everything they can to keep us hooked. You are going to feel strong urges, but take it one step at a time using the tips we have talked about. You are going to have good days and bad days, and that is okay.

People spend a lifetime trying to quit their drug addiction, and some are never successful. It took around nine months for me to stop feeling strong urges to use my phone. Your journey could be shorter than mine as I was actively experimenting with different techniques, or it could be longer, as we recognized how powerful a phone addiction can be in comparison to addictive drugs. Regardless of how long it takes you to break your addiction, don't get discouraged.

Conclusion

In case you aren't aware of the obvious, your time on this earth is finite. It is a scary thought, but recognizing this allows you to bring into focus how you should live your life. You should live it to the best of your ability, instead of being dragged around by a five-inch device that makes you unhappy, unhealthy, unproductive, and anxiety ridden. We have all allowed our lives to be dictated by massive corporations' desires that in no way reflect our own.

This book offers you a greater opportunity than simply using a device less. You can choose to read it and make none of the changes I have outlined but remember all the ways you could benefit. You gain over fifteen years of your life back; become more content, more confident, less anxious, more intelligent, more productive, and have better relationships. It gives you an opportunity to completely change the life you have been living. I hope breaking your phone addiction can create a better life for you like it has for me.

Jackson Antonow

Acknowledgments

I cannot emphasize the amount of gratitude I have for my friends and family who helped me throughout the process of writing this book. I said countless times while writing this book that I feel as if I barely wrote it and rather listened and transferred the experiences of my friends onto the pages. Writing a book was a daunting and unfamiliar task and something that aroused initial fears of failure and embarrassment. For those who supported me the entire time, I cannot be more grateful, as I might have quit if it wasn't for your support.

I first want to give special thanks to Will Moriarty, who created virtually every image in this book today (the pic of the model he did not create). These images took Will only seconds, as the skills it required to make these images were far below his capabilities. When Will is not helping me out, he creates sports video content for the Wisconsin Badgers that can be seen on willwmoriarty.com. His work is incredible.

Cole Tiran was instrumental in shepherding this book into a final product. Throughout the editing process, I received help from many smart and talented people like my editors Andrew Dawson and Ellen Tarlin, and my father, Chris Antonow, but Cole's perspective as a young person helped me elaborate on my ideas for my target audience. Cole is a great friend and also incredibly bright and insightful.

My father is the reason this book is what it is today. He is the smartest person I know, and to have such a valuable resource was the single most important factor, outside of myself, in the writing of this book. My father's commitment to tight editing schedules and his dedication to my passion is something for which I will forever be grateful. Besides his impact on this book, my father has supported me in every aspect of my life. Whether it be my education, sports, or hobbies, my father has put every ounce of himself into helping me succeed. I am extremely grateful for him and am so happy that he helped raised me.

I could not thank my father without also thanking my mother. While my mom was less hands on with the writing of this book, she gave me the confidence to believe in myself from a young age. Without this belief in myself, I don't know if I would have made the decision to write this book. I am so happy that my mother and father instilled in me the values I have today, and I truly think they are the most incredible parents in the world.

Throughout the book I talked about the effect Snapchat maps, response time, and social media had on me during my high school years. A lot of the quotes and experiences that I cited in this book came from direct conversations I had with Aydin Ozbek, Othel Owen, James Hanson, and Oliver Manilow. I am grateful for their openness, as it made me more open and allowed me to understand the emotions I was feeling weren't weak or unnatural.

There were other people I remember distinctly who helped me formulate specific thoughts in this book, such as Avi Colonomos, Julia Kibort, Emily Stoll, Ivy Jacobs, and Tony Fontana. I had conversations with them about wealth, sexualization, and experiencing social media as a woman, which I knew needed to be included but didn't know how to approach. Conversations with these five people are ultimately what formed those sections of the book.

I also want to thank the people who supported me unconditionally throughout this book and never once gave me a weird look when I explained to them what I was attempting to do. I remember every one of these conversations. These people were Sam Laser, Pierce Geene, Jonah Henschel, Jo Ho, Charlie Mihelic, Noah Davis, Colin Holt, Jayden Lott, Will Ates, Andreas Baechler, Luke Adams, Colin Dorsey, Alex Schapiro, Sam Meiselman-Ashen, Stratton Buck, Jalen Harris, E Antonow, Charlie Janson, P.J. Sitzer, Holden Knapp, and Michael Short. I am grateful for their support and grateful they are a part of my lives.

I would also like to thank David Hale Smith, an established literary agent with clients much more important than me, who took time out of his busy day to read and provide direction when this book was in its infancy.

I am appreciative for all the people who heard about my idea to write this book and went out of their way to let me know they supported what I was doing. I was getting used to negative responses when people found out I was writing this, but when I ran into Sam Shydlowski I received the exact opposite response. This moment truly made my day, as I could tell how much Sam appreciated what I was doing, and his sincerity was undeniable. His words gave me the extra motivation that I needed to finish this book.

As New York University business school professor Scott Galloway says, "People overestimate how integral they are to their own success." Without all of the people I mentioned, *Enemy in Your Pocket* would have never become a reality. For me to attempt to take sole credit for this book would a failure to recognize the people who helped me along the way. This would have never happened without all of you.

Endnotes

1. NHS (2021, May 9). *Addiction: What is it?* NHS Website. https://www.nhs.uk/live-well/addiction-support/addiction-what-is-it/#:~:text=Addiction%20is%20defined%20as%20not,could%20be%20harmful%20to%20you.
2. "Mobile Fact Sheet." Pew Research, 12 Dec. 2024, www.pewresearch.org/internet/fact-sheet/mobile/#:~:text=The%20vast%20majority%20of%20Americans,smartphone%20ownership%20conducted%20in%202011.&text=%25%20of%20U.S.%20adults%20who%20say%20they%20own%20a%20%E2%80%A6.
3. Taylor, Petroc. "U.S. Teen Smartphone Reach by Gender 2023." Statista, Statista, 28 Feb. 2024, www.statista.com/statistics/256501/teen-ceelphone-and-smartphone-ownership-in-the-us-by-gender/#:~:text=As%20of%20October%202023%2C%2097,had%20smartphone%20access%20at%20home.
4. O'Neill, Aaron. "United States - Age Distribution 2022." Statista, 4 July 2024, www.statista.com/statistics/270000/age-distribution-in-the-united-states/#:~:text=In%202022%2C%20about%2017.96%20percent,over%2065%20years%20of%20age.
5. Bureau, US Census. "Population." Census.Gov, United States Government, 22 July 2022, www.census.gov/topics/population.html.
6. Pottle, Z. (2024, May 12). 10 Most Common Addictions. *AddictionCenter*. https://www.addictioncenter.com/addiction/10-most-common-addictions/.
7. Smith, J. (2024, June 7). Tobacco Use Among Children and Teens. *American Lung Association*.

8. Reed, Susanne. "How Electronics Affect Sleep." *Sleep Foundation*, 2 Jun. 2023, www.sleepfoundation.org/how-sleep-works/how-electronics-affect-sleep. Accessed 10 Jun. 2024.
9. "Life Expectancy." *Centers for Disease Control and Prevention*, 2 May 2024, www.cdc.gov/nchs/fastats/life-expectancy.htm. Accessed 10 Jun. 2023.
10. Riedout, Victoria, et al. *The Common Sense Census: Media Use by Tweens and Teens*. Edited by Jennifer Robb, Common Sense Media, 2021.
11. "Looks Aren't Everything. Believe Me, I'm a Model." YouTube, uploaded by TED, 16 Nov. 2013, www.youtube.com/watch?v=KM4Xe6DlpOY.
12. "Study: False News Spreads Faster than Truth." *MIT Management Sloan School*, 8 May 2018, mitsloan.mit.edu/ideas-made-to-matter/study-false-news-spreads-faster-truth#:~:text=And%20false%20news%20reached%201%2C500,spread%20of%20false%20news%20online. Accessed 10 Jun. 2024.
13. Brown, G. (1994). Light, melatonin, and the sleep-wake cycle. *Journal of Psychiatry & Neuroscience*.
14. Pacheco, D. (2023, June 2). How Electronics Affect Sleep. *National Sleep Foundation*.
15. *The Social Dilemma*. Directed by Jeff Orlowski, Mass FX Media, 2018.
16. "Former Facebook Exec Says Social Media Is Ripping Apart Society." *The Verge*, 11 Dec. 2017, www.theverge.com/2017/12/11/16761016/former-facebook-exec-ripping-apart-society. Accessed 10 May 2024.
17. *The Social Dilemma*. Directed by Jeff Orlowski, Mass FX Media, 2018.
18. Haidt, Jonathan. *The Anxious Generation: How the Great Rewiring of Childhood Is Causing an Epidemic of Mental Illness*. Penguin Press, an Imprint of Penguin Random House LLC, 2024.
19. Chamberlin, Emma. "How Social Media Overwhelmed Me and My Solution." YouTube, 8 Sept. 2023, www.youtube.com/shorts/VNgIVYDOWw4.
20. TD Ameritrade ads; click on the website iSpot.tv. Once you are on the website, the advertisement is titled, "TD Ameritrade TV Spot, 'A Million Ways to Trade.'"
21. Jones, C. (2023, December 12). We're killing the youth of America: Calls grow for crackdown on US gambling. *The Guardian*. https://www.theguardian.com/us-news/2023/dec/01/sports-betting-regulation-gambling-addiction.
22. Haidt, Jonathan. *The Anxious Generation: How the Great Rewiring of Childhood Is Causing an Epidemic of Mental Illness*. Penguin Press, an Imprint of Penguin Random House LLC, 2024.
23. Eyal, Nir. *Indistractable: How to Control Your Attention and Choose Your Life*. Benbella Books, 2021.

Made in the USA
Columbia, SC
26 February 2025